A Sequel to The Night of Weeping

Joy comes in the morning.
—Psalm 30:5

The MORNING *of* JOY

Words of Cheer and Hope for the Bride of Christ

HORATIUS BONAR

We enjoy hearing from our readers. Please contact us at www.anekopress.com/questions-comments with any questions, comments, or suggestions.

Cover Designer: J. Martin

Cover Image: Volodymyr Martyniuk/Shutterstock

Editor: Paul Miller

Aneko Press

www.anekopress.com

Aneko Press, Life Sentence Publishing, and our logos are trademarks of

Life Sentence Publishing, Inc.
203 E. Birch Street
P.O. Box 652
Abbotsford, WI 54405

RELIGION / Christian Living / Inspirational

Paperback ISBN: 979-8-88936-276-0

eBook ISBN: 979-8-88936-277-7

10 9 8 7 6 5 4 3 2 1

Available where books are sold

Contents

Register This New Book

Benefits of Registering*

- ✓ FREE **replacements** of lost or damaged books

- ✓ FREE **audiobook** – *Pilgrim's Progress*, audiobook edition

- ✓ FREE information about new titles and other **freebies**

Preface

I have been asked several times to follow up *The Night of Weeping*[1] with *The Morning of Joy*. The words of David in Psalm 30 first suggested the addition, and after much thought and some hesitation, I have decided to write the book.

The previous work was meant to be complete in itself, presenting not merely the night view of tribulation, but also bringing out, though less prominently, some of the hues of day. However, as it has been thought incomplete, having in it so much more of night than of day, I have attempted to make it complete it by directing the eye to the scenes of morning, so soon to open upon us in all their breadth and beauty. In this way, we are led to forget the things that are behind, and to reach forward to those ahead, pressing toward the mark for the prize of our high calling (Philippians 3:13-14). The fuller, the truer, and the more frequent our anticipations of promised glory are, the deeper and the richer our consolations will be.

---

1   *The Night of Weeping* is a book written by Horatius Bonar and is available from Aneko Press.

Sitting down beneath the shadow of the cross and reading in its inscription God's record of free love, our fears are put to flight and our souls find rest. Possessed of forgiveness and assured of the life that does not die, we feel that all is well with us. We can say, "Come life or come death, come calm or storm, come gain or loss, come joy or grief – all is well," for *the work of righteousness will be peace, and the service of righteousness, quietness and confidence forever* (Isaiah 32:17).

Certainly this provides much in the way of comfort, even if we had nothing more to encourage us. But it is not all; there is much more than this.

While sitting there beneath the shadow of the cross, God shows us a wide view that stretches far into eternity. Perhaps He sends trial, breaking us with His tempest (Job 9:17). Then He spreads out before us the vision of brightness for our comfort, and as the grief presses heavier, the vision gets larger. The going down of our sun, even though it covers earth with a shadow, draws the curtain from the firmament above us and encircles us with the splendor of ten thousand stars. Then we not only are led to see that the greater portion of our being lies beyond either present joy or sorrow, but we are also led to inquire into those outlying hopes and to survey the whole breadth of that abundant inheritance of which we are the heirs.

As we will see, these inquiries and surveys are most blessed in their nature, and they are purifying, as well as comforting, in their tendency. They are filled with holiness and joy. They tend to make us forget the present in the future, and to acclimate us to the objects that have been so vividly presented to us. For, although it is true that "tears make the harvest of the heart to grow,"[2] yet it is the anticipated light of the unrisen morning that ripens it.

This is more than mere negative sympathy. It is positive and beneficial. The negative is: *Why should any living mortal, or any man, offer complaint?* (Lamentations 3:39) or *There the wicked cease from raging, and there the weary are at rest* (Job 3:17). As far as this goes, it is precious, but God has given us something more than this. The hope that He provides is not merely the hope of a quiet close to this world's weariness, but it is the hope of infinite gladness that is then to begin.

There is a passage in Job that exemplifies both of these very appropriately. Groaning under the pressure of no common grief, he cries out, *Oh that You would hide me in Sheol, that You would conceal me until Your wrath returns to You* (Job 14:13). It is as if he would be glad to be hidden anywhere, even in the grave, from such calamities. But then this is not enough. This is mere negative comfort. It is the mere cessation of suffering, and he is not content with this. He considers himself and cries out again: *That You would set a limit for me and remember me!* (Job 14:13).

He cannot bear the thought of always lying in the dust, even if it is a secure hiding place from the storms of earth. He does not want to be forgotten there. He would like to have a time set, at the end of which God might remember him. Then abruptly he asks, *If a man*

---

2   This is a line from the poem "The Voyage of St. Brendan" by Denis Florence MacCarthy (1817-1882).

dies, will he live again? Evidently answering himself, "Yes, he will live again," he calmly adds, *All the days of my struggle I will wait until my change comes* (Job 14:14).

It is a resurrection change that he looks for, and he rejoices in it as his hope. When that day arrives, the trumpet will sound, and the voice of God will speak, *You will call, and I will answer You* (Job 14:15). But how is he so assured of being remembered by God in this way? He knows how precious in His eyes even the dust of His saints is: *You will long for the work of Your hands* (Job 14:15).

Thus, although Job begins with what is merely negative – the ending of his grief and shame – he cannot rest there, but continues, in rapid hope, to the beginning of his joy and glory. It is the morning, with all its new life and reviving sunshine, that rises before his view and from far away pours into him its healing light.

The form of this world is passing away (1 Corinthians 7:31). This comforts us, for it assures us that no anguish will live long. But the form of *the world to come* (Hebrews 2:5) endures. This is exceptionally comforting, for all that that better age brings with it will abide forever. The inheritance is abundant, the city is joyful, the mansions are many, the title is sure, and the possession is everlasting. One of Scotland's holiest sons in the olden time sweetly sung:

> *Jerusalem! Jerusalem!*
>   *Would God I were in thee!*
> *Oh that my sorrows had an end,*
>   *Thy joys that I might see.*[3]

---

3   This is a stanza from the hymn "Jerusalem, My Happy Home."

Broken with many griefs, he thus poured out his soul, weary and homesick, as a stranger here. And will not night fail in one of its plans if it does not make us long for day? Will not tribulation be discontent if it does not stir within us this *anxious longing* (Romans 8:19), this groaning *within ourselves* (Romans 8:23), this fervent longing – this homesickness that the saints in other days felt so tenderly and truly? And all the more, *for now salvation is nearer to us than when we believed* (Romans 13:11). We have arrived at the last stage of our journey, and a few more days will be sufficient to bring us home.

Horatius Bonar

Kelso, Scotland

December 19, 1849

Chapter 1

The Anticipations

The church of God on earth is not what she seems; rather, it is what she does not seem to be. She is not a beggar, yet she seems to be one. She is a King's bride, yet she does not seem to be. It was the same way with her Lord while He was here. He was not what people thought He was. Rather, He was what they did not think Him to be.

It is in this way that the world is put to shame, its thoughts confounded, and its greatness diminished before God. It is in this way that divine wisdom gets much room over which to spread itself, step by step, and to open its infinite resources slowly and with care (like someone displaying his treasures) so that no part, no turn in all its windings, may be left unobserved. It is not only the result that God desires that we should see and wonder at, but also the process by which it is reached, so unlikely to achieve it, yet so steadily moving forward to its end, and so remarkably successful in bringing about that end. The planting of the trees of God in Eden, in full strength and fruitfulness at once, was not such an exhibition of wisdom as that which we ourselves see in yearly process before us when God brings a stately pine or palm tree out of a small, shapeless seed.

In truth, this is the law of our world. It might not have been so at first in Eden, when only the result was seen, but it has been this way since, and it is this way now, for God is showing us most precisely how *fearfully and wonderfully* all things are made (Psalm 139:14), and we among the rest, in soul and in body, in our first birth and in our second, in our natural and in our spiritual growth.

In winter, the tree is not what it appears – dead; rather, it is what it does not appear to be – alive. It is full in every part – root, stem, and branch – of vigorous though hidden vitality, a vitality that frosts and storms are only maturing rather than quenching.

In winter, the tree is not what it appears...

All summer life is there and all autumn fruitfulness is there, though neither is visible. It wraps up within itself the seeds of future vegetation and awaits the coming spring. It is the same with the church in this age of wintry night, for it is both night and winter with her. Her present condition hardly agrees with her future. No one, by looking at her, could guess what she either is or is to be. No one, by looking at her, could conceive what God has in store for her. Eye has nothing to do with the seeing of it, nor ear with the hearing of it. No one, in observing her apparel or her manner, or the treatment she receives at the hands of men, or the sharp, heavy discipline through which she is passing, could fathom the magnitude of her hopes. Faith finds difficulty in realizing her future, and she can hardly at times credit the greatness of her heritage when thinking of what she is and remembering what she has been.

It often seems strange to us, and it must seem much more so to unfallen beings, that saints would be found at all in such a world – a world without God, a world of atheists, a world that from the days of Cain has rejected His Son, both as the sacrifice for sin and as the heir of all things. It is not on such a spot that we should naturally expect to find children of God. Next to hell, it is the unlikeliest place for a soul that loves God to dwell in, even for a day. If a stranger were traveling across the universe in search of God's little flock, His chosen ones, and were to ask us where God's flock was to be found, certainly he would be astonished when told that they were in that very world where Satan reigned and from which God had been cast out! He would say, "Either this is a mistake and an accident, or else it is the very depth of unfathomable wisdom." We do not go to the crater's slope for lush foliage, nor for flowers to the desert, nor for the plants of heaven to the shores of the lake of fire; yet it is so with the church. It might be strange to find a Joseph in Egypt, a Rahab in Jericho, or an Obadiah in the house of Ahab – but it is more amazing to find saints in the world at all. Yet they are here.

In spite of everything hostile in soil and air, they are here. They never seem to become acclimated, yet they do not die out, but are ever renewed. The enemy labors to uproot them, but they are deep-rooted. They thrive and bear fruit. It is a miracle, yet so it is. Here the great Husbandman is cultivating His plants from generation to generation. Here the great Potter forms His vessels. Here the great Master Builder cuts and polishes the stones for His eternal temple.

Therefore, one characteristic of the church is the unlikeliness of her present condition in comparison to her future condition. It is this that marks her out, that isolates her, as a gem in the heart of a rock or as a vein of gold in a mine. Originally she belonged to the large mass, but she was drawn apart from it, or it fell off from her and left her alone, like a pillar among ruins. Outwardly she retains much of her former self, but inwardly she has undergone a change that has familiarized her with *the world to come* (Hebrews 2:5). Therefore, her affections and her sympathies are all with that better world. Her dwelling is still here, and in external appearance she is much as she used to be, but the internal transformation has made her feel that this is not her home. She is filled with anticipations of the city and the kingdom to come, of which she has been made the heir. Her kindred according to the flesh are here, but she is now allied to Jehovah by the ties of blood, and this draws her soul upward.

Cut off from a home and a heritage here, yet assured of both in the future, she of necessity lives a life of anticipation. Giving credit to the message of grace, and resting on the blood of Him through whose cross that grace came down to her, she anticipates her acquittal at the judgment. Realizing her oneness with the risen and ascended Christ, she feels as if she is already seated with Him in heavenly places (Ephesians 2:6). Looking forward to the arrival of the King, she anticipates the kingdom. In darkness, she anticipates the light; in sorrow, she anticipates the joy; in the night, she anticipates the morning; in shame, she anticipates the glory. She understands the truth about her: *All things belong to you, whether Paul or Apollos or Cephas or the world or life or death or things present or things to come; all things belong to you, and you belong to Christ; and Christ belongs to God* (1 Corinthians 3:21-23). In these *My treasure is in heaven.* anticipations, she lives. They make up a large portion of her daily being. They encourage her onward in spite of the rough wildernesses she has to pass through. They comfort her, or when they do not quite succeed in this, they at least calm and soothe her. They do not turn midnight into noon, but they make it less oppressive and take off "the night side of nature."[4]

She says to herself, "I am not what I seem, and this brings joy. I am not the impoverished outcast that the world takes me for. I am far richer than they are. They have their riches now, but mine are coming when theirs are gone. They have their joys now, but mine are coming when theirs have ended in eternal weeping. I live in the future. My treasure is in heaven, and my heart has gone up to be where my treasure is. I will soon be seen to be what I now do not seem to be. My kingdom is at

---

4   *The Night-Side of Nature* is the title of a book written by Catherine Crowe that was published in 1848.

hand. My sun is about to rise. I will soon *see the King in His beauty* (Isaiah 33:17). I will soon be celebrating, and the joy of my promised morning will make me forget that I ever wept."

She lives in the morning before the morning has come. She takes a wide look all around, without any limitation, for faith has no horizon. It looks beyond life and earth and the ages into eternity.

Beyond the deathbed and the grave, she sees resurrection. Beyond the broken hearts and severed cords of time, she realizes and clasps the eternal links of love. She looks beyond the troubles of the hour and beyond the storm that is to wreck the world, and she feels as if transported into the kingdom that cannot be moved, as if she had already taken up her abode in the new Salem, the city of peace and righteousness. Beyond the region of the falling leaf, she moves on to the green pastures and sits down under the branches of the Tree of Life, which is in the midst of the paradise of God (Revelation 2:7). Losing sight of the bitterness of absence from the Beloved of her heart, she enters the bridal chamber and feels the bridal joy, rejoicing even in the desert, and enjoying the sabbath rest amid the turmoil of a stormy world.

Chapter 2

The Night Watch

We are not of the world, even though we are in the world (John 17:16). In the same way, we are not of the night, even though we are in the night. We are children of the day (1 Thessalonians 5:5). We belong to the day, and the day belongs to us, as our true heritage, although it has not yet dawned. Hope rests there, and although it is deferred, it will one day arrive – and when it comes, it will not shame our trust. *Desire fulfilled is a tree of life* (Proverbs 13:12).

Night is still around us, but it is not merely one of weeping; it is also one of watching. No sorrow is to make us less watchful, but should make us much more watchful. So far from tribulation throwing us off our guard, it should lead to added vigilance. It prevents us from falling asleep, as we would certainly do if all were peaceful and prosperous. It makes the night more cold and bitter to us, thereby rendering us more weary of it and more eager for the day. If the night air were mild and the night sky clear, we would grow content with it and would cease to watch for daybreak.

This is our night watch. The Master has appointed us to this during His absence. *Therefore, be on the alert—for you do not know when the master of the house is coming, whether in the evening, at midnight,*

The Master has appointed us to this during His absence.

or when the rooster crows, or in the morning—in case he should come suddenly and find you asleep. What I say to you I say to all, "Be on the alert!" (Mark 13:35-37). It is the anticipation of morning and of the Master's return that keeps us watching, especially in these last days – when watch after watch has come and gone, and He has not yet arrived. *His going forth is as certain as the dawn* (Hosea 6:3), and that morning cannot now be distant.

The church must fulfill her night watch. Whether long or short, perilous or easy, she must fulfill it. She is specifically called to watch, and she will sadly dishonor her profession, as well as disobey her Lord, if she does not watch. She does not need to consider substituting other duties for this as more needful, more important, or more in character. She does not dare to say, "I love, I believe, I pray, and I praise. Why should I also watch? Will not these do just as well as watching, or is not watching included in these?" Her Lord has told her to watch, and no other duty, no other grace, can be a substitute or an excuse for this.

She is to believe, but that is not all; she is also to watch. She is to rejoice, but that is not all; she is also to watch. She is to love, but that is not all; she is also to watch. She is to wait, but that is not all; she is also to watch. She is to hope, but that is not all; she is also to watch. This is to be her special attitude, and nothing can compensate for it. She is to be known in all ages as the watching one. By this the world is to be made to feel the difference between itself and her. By this she is specifically to show how truly she feels herself to be a stranger here.

People ask her, *Why do you stand looking into the sky?* (Acts 1:11). Her reply is, "I am watching." People mock her and say, "Why this activity?" Her reply is, "I am watching." People think it is strange that she does not *run with them into the same excesses of dissipation* (1 Peter 4:4). She tells them, "I am watching." They ask her to come forth and join their fun, to go out and sing their songs, to take part in their pleasures so that they may teach her to forget her sorrows. She refuses, saying, "I dare not; I am watching." The scoffer mocks her and says, *Where is the promise of His coming?* (2 Peter 3:4). She pays no attention to him, but continues watching and clings to her hope more firmly.

Sometimes a feeble, doubting, or inconsistent saint asks in wonder, "How are you so strong, so resilient, so able for the struggle, and so successful in the battle?" She answers, "I watch." Or he asks, "How do you keep up a spirit so elevated and maintain a walk so close, so consistent, so unearthly?" She answers, "I watch." Or he asks, "How do you overcome laziness, selfishness, and love of ease? How do you suppress worry and anxiety, or gain the victory over a contrary spirit?" She answers, "I watch." He asks, "How do you make progress against your fears? How do you face danger, defy enemies, and keep the flesh under control?" She replies, "I watch." Or he asks, "How do you wrestle with your griefs, dry up your tears, heal your wounds, and even glory in tribulation?" She answers, "I watch."

Oh, what this watching can do to one who understands it properly! Faith alone will not do. Love alone will not do. Expectation alone will not do. Obedience alone will not do. There must be watching.

This watching takes for granted the suddenness and uncertainty of the day of the Lord. It does not say that the Lord *must* come in my day, but it says that the Lord *may* come in my day, and that is why I must be watching. This "may come" is the secret of a watchful spirit. We cannot watch without it. We may love and hope and wait, but we cannot watch. Our lamps are to be always trimmed. Why? It is not merely because the Bridegroom is to come, but because we do not know how soon He may come. We are always to be *dressed in readiness* (Luke 12:35). Why? It is not simply because we know that He will be coming, but because we do not know when that coming is to be.

The Lord knew about the spirit of unwatchfulness into which His people would be inclined to fall while He tarried, and He warns us against it. He wants us to always remember that there will be a danger of our becoming careless and worldly: content with His absence instead of mourning because of it; content with His delay instead of joining in the ancient cry, *How long?* (Psalm 13:1). He saw that the world would throw us off our guard, that few people would really keep awake and watch, that many people would get tired of watching and would make excuses for not watching, and that many people would sit down and try to make themselves comfortable here without Him. That is why He so often repeated the warning, "Watch!" That is why He added, *in case he should come suddenly and find you asleep* (Mark 13:35-36).

His desire is that we should be watching so well that when He comes and knocks, we may *immediately open the door* (Luke 12:36). He pronounces a special blessing upon those servants whom He finds doing so, promising that *he will gird himself to serve, and have them recline at the table, and will come up and wait on them* (Luke 12:37). To be in such an attitude of watchfulness that we will be ready to open the door to Him immediately is that to which He has promised so special a reward and so wondrous an honor.

Who among us is in this condition in these last days? Would we be ready to open the door to Him immediately if He arrived now? Would we not be thrown into confusion at the news of His coming, like servants unprepared for their master's return, and not counting on it so soon? Would we not have to get ready when we should be opening the door? Would we not have to run to put on our necessary and proper garments instead of going forth to welcome Him? What confusion in the household, what amazement, what fear, what bustle, what running to and fro would there be in our day if the news would be brought to us that the Lord has come!

In the repeated command to watch, there is much

rebuke. The Lord could not trust us to remember it for ourselves or to obey instinctively. If He had been able to count on perfect love in us to Himself – love full and deep like His own – would He have thought of such a command? Would it have been needed? No, it would not have been needed. All that would have been needed would have been to tell us that He intended to return. Love would have supplied the rest, and of itself, would have made us watchful. Love would have made it impossible that it should be otherwise. It would have needed neither the command nor the declaration of uncertainty and suddenness. It would have anticipated all these. It would have acted without having to be asked. However, the Lord could not trust us. He could not trust our love, and therefore He added the command and repeated the warning. It is strange and sad indeed that neither the power of love nor the significance of the command can awaken us into watchfulness or motivate us into preparation.

The announcements of the suddenness of His coming are very distinct and specific. There is nothing vague about them. There is nothing to take off the edge of the warning that they contain. They are much more specific and repeated than those of His first coming. His first coming took the church by surprise, even though He had set the time and had numbered the years. How much more, then, is His second coming likely to surprise us when, by the way in which He has announced it, He has prevented us from counting on any interval at all! Yet we do not watch! Neither His measuring the time in the one case, nor His leaving it unmeasured in the other, produces the appropriate response. *When the Son of Man comes, will He find faith on the earth?* (Luke 18:8).

During this time of our night watch, faith is to be constantly vigorous and in motion, for it is the root of watchfulness. Without faith, one can hardly have the idea of what it is to watch, for all the objects toward which watchfulness turns are connected with things unseen – an unseen Savior and an unseen kingdom.

When we first knew the Lord and believed on Him as the peacemaker, not only were we freely forgiven, but we were also delivered from a present evil world. Things present fell away from us, and things to come gathered around us. What was once shadowy became real, and what once seemed real seemed then like a shadow. Christ's words became real words, His

Without faith, one can hardly have the idea of what it is to watch.

truths became real truths, and His promises became real promises to us. Everything else appeared unreal. The veil was not withdrawn, but we realized what was within it. The future did not become the present, nor the invisible the visible, but we felt as if they were so. Our faith was *the assurance of things hoped for, the conviction of things not seen* (Hebrews 11:1). Believing, then, that the Lord is coming, that the time is short, that the interval is uncertain, and that His arrival will be sudden, we watch. Unbelief throws us off our guard, but faith sends us to our watchtower. We know what our Lord meant when He said, *Blessed are they who did not see, and yet believed* (John 20:29).

Altering the words of our Lord, may we not also say, "Blessed are they who have seen and yet have not believed"? To see and yet not to believe is one of the things that faith teaches us, and is one of the things that awaken watchfulness. We look upon a world full of ungodliness, yet do not believe that God has forsaken the earth. We see the world's wisdom worshiped, yet do not believe that it is wisdom. We see the power of evil, yet do not believe that evil will triumph. We see confusion everywhere, yet do not believe that order is not God's law. We see a divided church, yet we believe that the church is one. We see mighty kingdoms ruling, yet do not believe that they will remain. We see the saints trodden down, yet do not believe in their shame or extinction. We look upon the tomb of the righteous, yet do not believe that he is dead. We see the church's persecutions and defeats, yet we believe not only that she is conqueror, but invincible. We see the march of Antichrist, yet do not believe in his progress, except as a progression to destruction. We see the world's joy, yet do not believe that it is joy. We see the saint's sorrow, yet do not believe that he is sorrowful. We see night – thick, deep night – around us, yet we do not believe in the night, but in the day.

Therefore, faith triumphs. We believe, we trust, and we hope; and in doing so, we stand above the world. We lift up our eyes to the hills, from where our help comes (Psalm 121:1). We look toward the east, where the dawn breaks. We watch for the morning. Our night watch has been long and weary, but the morning will soon end it. The watching, the waiting, and the hoping will then be done, but the loving will be forever.

We watch, for we know of no interval between us and the Lord's appearing. The hour of our meeting with Him, and with those whom we have loved and lost, may be close at hand. Sooner than we think, we may be joined together inseparably – our bodies clothed with resurrection health, and our souls rejoicing in holiness and love.

We watch, for it is night, and although we are not children of the night, still the night with its shadows rests heavily upon us, making us look with eager desire for its passing. We grow more dissatisfied with it as it deepens. It brings so many griefs, it gathers around us so many temptations, it calls up so many dangers, and it gives courage to so many enemies that we grow troubled that it lasts so long; yet we cannot make it go away. God's purpose must be served, and His time must be spent. Until then, let us possess our souls in patience while watching for dayspring and stirring up our souls with the assurance that we know of nothing between us and the ending of our long night watch.

We watch, for the day is ours, with all that it contains of gladness and sunshine. We are weary of the night, and we rejoice that it is not ours, although we are in it – but we rejoice that the day is ours. Just as we can say, "The kingdom is ours," so we can say, "The day is ours," and we watch for it as being ours. Its light is ours. Its blue sky is ours. Its mild air is ours. Its cheerful sounds are ours. Its friendly greetings are ours. All that it calls forth of joy and health and purity are ours.

Does anyone need to wonder that we would watch for such a day?

We watch, for the night is far spent. Not only do we know of nothing before us before the Lord arrives, but we know of much behind us. Hours, years, and ages have gone by, and if the whole night was to be brief – only a "little while – then certainly very much of it must now be over. *The night is almost gone*, says the apostle (Romans 13:12). Literally, it is "cut off." It is shortened. It is becoming shorter. It is drawing to a close.

Behind us are centuries of tears and shadows. The greater part of the little while must be past. The day must be near. The nearness makes the thought of day doubly welcome. We lean toward it with warm longings. We strain our eyes to catch the first sign of it. We stir up ourselves to vigilance, knowing that *now salvation is nearer to us than when we believed* (Romans 13:11).

How it disappoints, how it disheartens, to be told that there are centuries more of this night watching still to come! If that could be proved, it would sadly dampen our hope. We might at once come down from our watchtower and give up our expectations. To look for and hasten the coming of the day of God (2 Peter 3:12) would no longer be a duty. The last generation of the church, living at the close of the millennium, might get up into the watchtower, but for us, watching would be a name, a mere attitude of form or show.

By looking and praying and watching, we hasten that day, even though it is determined by the purpose of God – just as we are instruments (by prayer, etc.) in the conversion of a friend, although that also depends on the purpose of God.

It has always been Satan's purpose to interject some object between the church and her Lord's arrival, but never did he come upon a more deceptive, more successful device than that of making the interjected object a glorious and blessed one. The church would not have listened to any other kind. She would have withdrawn and turned away from a thousand years' sorrow, but she is attracted and fascinated by the promise of a thousand years' rest and joy.

It has always been Satan's purpose to interject some object between the church and her Lord's arrival.

Yet is the interjection of any fixed interval (whether sad or joyous) lawful or scriptural? If the Lord's coming is thrust into the distance, it does not matter what may be introduced to fill the interval. If the hope of the church is hidden, it is not important whether it is hidden by a shroud of sackcloth or by a veil of woven gold.

God deals with the church as one. Although the church consists of many generations, God looks upon it as one body. In reference to her hope, He has so formed His revelation that every generation of the church should stand upon the same footing as the last. How has this been done? How has the first age, and how have all subsequent ages, been placed in the same position as the last? This was accomplished by simply concealing the interval. In this thing it has been truly *the glory of God to conceal a matter* (Proverbs 25:2). It is by this method, so simple and so natural, that each age of the church has been made to feel precisely as the last will feel; that they will watch just as the last age will watch – when the Lord is truly at hand.

So it is that this body, which is spread over centuries, has at all times been made to occupy a position and present a character that is the same as if it had been a body whose life and actions were summed up in one generation. Therefore, any known interval introduced before the coming of the Lord alters the posture, destroys the character, and breaks the oneness of the church, while it defeats the purpose that God had so specifically in view in keeping the times and seasons in His own power.

Since the Lord left the earth, the watch has often been changed and the guard relieved. God has not tried too severely the faith of any one age by making the watch too long. In mercy, He has cut down man's age from patriarchal longevity to seventy years (Psalm 90:10) lest the overwearied watchers would collapse under the toil and hardship. It is this that makes unwatchfulness so inexcusable. Adam or Seth or Methuselah or Noah might have had the edge of their watchfulness blunted by the long conflict of nine hundred years, but what excuse do we have for carelessness! Our time of service is brief, and to fall asleep or to grow impatient would indicate sad apathy and unfaithfulness. *You men could not keep watch with Me for one hour? Keep watching and praying that you may not enter into temptation* (Matthew 26:40-41). If the Lord does not come in our day by His personal presence to end our watching, we still cannot complain of exhaustion or being burned out since we will be so soon relieved and taken into His nearer presence, there to watch in rest and joy and light, as here we have watched in weariness and grief and darkness.

As Edward Irving wrote in his *Lectures on the Revelation* (vol. 1, p. 77):

> Blessed conclusion of this weary and sorrowful world! I welcome it. I hail its approach. I wait for its coming more than they who watch for the morning. Over the desolation of a world, I weep – over broken hearts of parents, over suffering infancy, over the unconscious clay of sweet innocents, over the untimely births that have never seen the light, or have just looked upon it and shut their eyes for a season, until the glorious light of the resurrection morn.

> O my Lord, come away! Hasten with all Your congregated ones. My soul desires to see the King in His beauty, and the beautiful ones whom He shall bring along with Him – when I shall see these sweet babes, snatched from a parent's weeping eyes, and a parent's sorrowful yet joyful heart.

Chapter 3

The Foretastes of the Morning

The true morning has not yet broken. It hardly gives forth any sign of breaking other than the deeper darkness that is the sure foreteller of the dawn.

It is still night upon the earth; and the children of the night are going to and fro in the world's streets, doing *the unfruitful deeds of darkness* (Ephesians 5:11); *having pursued a course of sensuality, lusts, drunkenness, carousing, drinking parties and abominable idolatries* (1 Peter 4:3); yielding to the *flattering lips* of the seducer (Proverbs 7:21), who *lurks by every corner* (Proverbs 7:12) *in the middle of the night and in the darkness* (Proverbs 7:9); making provision for the flesh by carousing and drunkenness, in sexual promiscuity and sensuality, and in strife and jealousy (Romans 13:13-14); and surrounding themselves with sparks of their own kindling, which only sadden the gloom and make us feel more truly that it is night.

It is still night to the church. It is a night of danger,

a night of weariness, and a night of weeping. Her sky is dark and troubled. The promise of morning is certain, and she is looking out for it with focused and pleading eye, severely tried with the long gloom, yet it has not arisen. It is still delayed – delayed in mercy to an unready world, to whom the ending of this night will be the closing of hope, the sealing of ruin, and the settling down of the infinite darkness. *The Lord is not slow about His promise, as some count slowness, but is patient toward you, not wishing for any to perish but for all to come to repentance* (2 Peter 3:9).

The promise of morning is certain.

Although it is night, there are times both in the saint's own history and in the church's history that may be spoken of as mornings even now. Such was the "morning" to Adam when Seth was born to him after Abel's death (Genesis 4:25). Such was the "morning" to Noah when the flood dried up and the face of the earth was renewed (Genesis 8). Such was the "morning" to Jacob when the news came to him that Joseph was still alive (Genesis 45:26-28). Such was the "morning" to Naomi when Ruth and Boaz wiped off the tears of widowhood, and when in her old age she saw her seed and *took the child and laid him in her lap* (Ruth 4:16). Such was Hannah's "morning" when, after long years of bitterness, the Lord granted her petition, and she *went her way and ate, and her face was no longer sad* (1 Samuel 1:18). Such was the "morning" that dawned on Job when the Lord accepted him and turned his captivity, giving him twice as much as he had before. *The Lord blessed the latter days of Job more than his beginning* (Job 42:12).[5] Such was Israel's "morning" when the Lord turned back the captivity of Zion, making them *like those who dream*, filling their mouths with laughter and their tongues with singing in the day of their deliverance from exile (Psalm 126:1-2).

We see, then, that there are "mornings" now and then bursting upon us now. They are indeed little more than brief glows in the darkness – lulls in the long tempest that is to rage unspent until the Lord comes. Yet we may still call them "mornings," just as we give the name of midday to the dim glow of the sky at daily noon during the six months' arctic night when the sun remains below the horizon. Or better and truer, we may call them foretastes of the morning – that morning that is to outshine all mornings and will swallow up both the darkness and the light of a present evil world. As dim and brief as these foretastes are, they are inexpressibly encouraging. They calm the heavy darkness and are pledges of sunrise.

Our life on earth, the life that we now live in the flesh (Galatians 2:20), is thus made up of many nights and many mornings. It is not all one night, nor is it all one day. Everything pertaining to it seems to revolve or change. It is a life of sinking and rising, of going and returning, of ebbing and flowing, and of shade and brightness. The health of the soul seems in some

---

5   Yet even here there seems to be an allusion to the true morning yet to come, and an intimation that all this restored fullness was only a foretaste, for while Job has all his sheep, oxen, etc. exactly doubled to him, his children are not doubled. He lost seven, and he gets back seven, for he must look to the resurrection morning for restoration of his seven lost ones, and not until then is he to get the double.

measure to need such changes, just as the soil owes much of its fruitfulness to the changes of the seasons.

Just as there is no steady continuance of constant good, so there is no equal pressure of unbroken evil. Just as the season of calm is brief, so is the burst of the storm. The days of darkness are many – more in number than the days of light – yet they do not last forever. *Many are the afflictions of the righteous*, yet there are gaps in the line of evil, for it is added that *the Lord delivers him out of them all* (Psalm 34:19).

Our God has so made us, and so directed our circumstances, that each grief has its crisis, its flood tide, after which it seems, as if by a law, to recede. Not only can the soul not bear more than a fixed amount of pain or pressure without giving way, but it cannot be strained for too long. If the straining is prolonged, the spirit fails and the mind breaks down. Or if this is not the case, we grow indifferent, cold, and numb. Affliction loses its power by being too heavy or too long.

The highest mountain has its summit, and the deepest mineshaft has its lowest level, and in general, it does not take long to reach these. So even when there is sorrow upon sorrow, there is relief between, or gladness at the close of the dark series. To some extent, the outer and the inner world have the same laws of succession and relief. Tides and variations seem necessary in both.

This is how it was in the life of David. At one time he stood with gladness in the courts of his God, and at another time he grieved for himself, saying, *When shall I come and appear before God?* (Psalm 42:2). At one time he went with the multitude, and at another time he wandered in solitude and exile. At one time he kept a holy day with the thousands of Israel, joining in the voice of joy and praise, and at another time his tears were his food day and night (Psalm 42:3). At one time his soul was cast down and disquieted within him (Psalm 42:5, 11), and at another time he praised Jehovah as the health of his countenance (Psalm 42:11). At one time he could look with an open eye upon the glory of Jehovah in His house, and at another time he could only remember Him *from the land of Jordan and the peaks of Hermon, from Mount Mizar* (Psalm 42:6). At one time deep called unto deep, and all God's waves went over him, and at another time the Lord commanded His lovingkindness and opened his mouth in song (Psalm 42:7-8). Such were the tides of David's history – the fluctuations of day and night in his varying journey.

This is true of every saint's history, not only in the old age of shadows, but also in our own! This is an accurate example of the changes and tossings marked out for the church in her course on earth from shame to glory! What else are we to look for until the Lord comes? In the first age of the church, in the time of righteous Abel, it was so. *There was evening and there was morning, one day* (Genesis 1:5). In the last age of the church, just before the second Adam is brought in, it will be no less so. *There was evening and there was morning, the sixth day* (Genesis 1:31). Then comes the world's seventh and brightest day – a day of cloudless splendor, unbroken and unending.

How wise, how gracious that it should be so! One

firmament of gloom that spans our whole lifetime would be intolerable. One long heavy chain of grief, with which we could never get comfortable, and on which we could never learn to look calmly; or one linked succession of griefs, always tearing open old wounds and adding new ones, would wither up existence and devastate life before its prime. Man's nature could not bear it. Man's heart would sink under it, unless made totally callous by some unnatural process, or sustained by daily miracle – in which case grief would cease to be grief, and there could be no such thing as trial or chastisement at all.

Therefore, He who *knows our frame [and] is mindful that we are but dust* (Psalm 103:14) not only halts His fierce wind in the day of the east wind (Isaiah 27:8), but often, for a time, commands both to be still, and breathes on us only with the freshness of the mild south. For He has said, *I will not contend forever, nor will I always be angry; for the spirit would grow faint before Me, and the breath of those whom I have made* (Isaiah 57:16). This, then, is God's purpose concerning us, and these are His reasons for it. The purpose is a gracious and a tender one, and the reasons for it are no less so. He tells us that although at times He does contend with us, yet He will not prolong the contest beyond a certain time or limit; for in such a strife, who could stand before the Mighty One? God contended with them in measure (Isaiah 27:8); that is, He will set limits to the sorrow and the affliction that cannot be crossed. He will say to them, even in their fiercest course, *Thus far you shall come, but no farther* (Job 38:11). If He were to allow that tide to roll on unhindered, who, even of His own chosen and beloved ones, could withstand its rush or sustain themselves amid its deepening waters?

Yet let us not forget what the sorrow has done for us while it lasted, and what the night has been, although dark and sad. It has been a night of grief, yet a night of blessing. It has been a night in which there may have been many things that we wish we could forget, yet with many more things that we would want to remember forever. Often, during its gloom, we called it wearisome and said, *When I lie down I say, "When shall I arise?"*

Let us not forget what the sorrow has done for us while it lasted.

But the night continues, and I am continually tossing until dawn (Job 7:4). Yet how much there was to reconcile us to it, and even to fill us with praise because of it! It was then that the Lord drew near. It was then that the world was removed from our hearts, self was smitten, our will was conquered, faith grew quickly, hope became brighter and more fervent, and the things that are unseen were felt to be real and true. Jerusalem that is above was seen by us as our proper home.

It was then that we had *songs in the night* (Job 35:10). Our minds instructed us in the *night* (Psalm 16:7). It was in the night that we remembered the name of our God (Psalm 119:55) and our souls longed for Him (Isaiah 26:9), meditating on Him in the night watches (Psalm 63:6). It was in the night that He led us *with a light of fire* (Psalm 78:14). It was in the night that the dew lay upon our branch (Job 29:19), and with the dew there came down the manna, for the manna and the dew fell together (Numbers 11:9) so that out of the heart of the darkness there came at the same time nourishment and freshness. It was then that we were taught sympathy with a groaning creation, taking part in its anxious longing (Romans 8:19) and waiting for resurrection, even as it is looking out for redemption. It was then that we were taught to know our high office, as those who have the firstfruits of the Spirit, "to lead," as Edward Irving wrote, "the choir of all-complaining nature," for it was then that the Spirit's power came forth upon us to tune the chords of our diverse being so that they might give forth the true note of mingled hope and sadness, distinct to creation in its present low condition; and when we were grumbling under the touch, and perhaps, with sentimental weakness, talking about broken strings and a hopeless life, the hand of the great Master Tuner was upon us, giving to each rebellious chord its proper tension so that from the retuned instrument there might come forth that special harmony that He desires to draw from it in this present age – that special harmony by which He is to be glorified on earth until Eden comes again and the wilderness blossoms as the rose (Isaiah 35:1).

It was then that we could make the utterance of Jacob's patient faith our own: *For Your salvation I wait, O LORD* (Genesis 49:18), joining ourselves to our fellow saints as *your brother and fellow partaker in the tribulation and kingdom and perseverance which are in Jesus* (Revelation 1:9) – that is, in patiently waiting for His kingdom. It was then that these words of blessed cheer fell so sweetly on our ears: *He who testifies to these things says, "Yes, I am coming quickly,"* drawing forth from our lips the glad response, *Amen. Come, Lord Jesus* (Revelation 22:20). And it was then that, while learning in this way to plead, *Hasten* (Psalm 70:1), we also learned to say with the Bride, *My beloved is to me a pouch of myrrh which lies all night between my breasts* (Song of Solomon 1:13).

As blessed and profitable, however, as we have found the night with its still seclusion and solemn teachings, it is not the morning or the day. Its very darkness makes us long even more for the anticipated sunrise – when the shadows flee away and the eternal day breaks.

Nor are we hindered from desiring the day. Impatience is forbidden, but desire is not. Let us possess our souls in patience (Luke 21:19), for he is neither a brave or believing man who says, "Let me die, for the cup is bitterer than I can drink." Rather, he is brave and believing who can say under the severest trial, "Let me live on and be useful, no matter how bitter the cup may be." But still we may desire the night to end. Just as in sickness we may long for health and put forth all proper means to attain it, so in darkness we may cry earnestly for the dawning, especially because we know that God has a day in store for us after the night is done – a day that is to be far more than a compensation for all previous sorrow. For every night, God has provided a morning, so that just as we have many nights here, we also have many mornings here. They are not indeed mornings without clouds (2 Samuel 23:4), but still they are mornings whose cheerful light lifts up the heavy spirit and brightens the dim eye.

However, for the world, the children of the night, the heedless, pleasure-loving world – what morning is there, or what foretaste of the morning? None, or at least it does not deserve the name of morning. Their sorrows are multiplied because they have hastened after other gods (Psalm 16:4). Their joy is only for a moment. Their consolation is no better than a dream. They serve a god that cannot save and that cannot comfort. Their portion here at the best is emptiness, and the end is eternal blackness and infinite despair. They do not regard the tidings of God's free love, but before long they will be made to regard the tidings of His wrath – if now they do not turn to Him who is requesting of them this one favor, that they would bring their sins to Him for forgiveness and let Him bear all their griefs and carry all their sorrows.

Chapter 4

The Use of These Foretastes

"**N**ow for a swifter race!" was the resolve of one over whose path sorrow was beginning to darken heavily. "Now for a busier and more useful life!" was the utterance of another as he rose from his knees after pouring out the bitterness of his grief into the ear of God.

In these cases, tribulation was taking its true course and working its right end. It had gone down to the most sacred depths of the renewed heart and was calling up buried feelings of devotedness that had remained dormant, but not extinct, under a heap of worldliness. It smote our selfishness, our narrow-mindedness, our laziness, and our pleasing of the flesh, and it reminded us that we had no time to waste or to sleep. Tearing off the veil that prosperous days had flung over our eyes, it pointed to the vanity of things seen and temporal (2 Corinthians 4:18), until the vastness of the unseen and the eternal grew upon us so much that we rose up and went forth, resolving on a swifter race and a busier life on earth.

Still there was a hindrance. The very trial that stirred us up also weighed us down, unraveling our strength and nearly causing us to faint. The pressure slowed our swiftness, and the deep wound, still bleeding, weakened us. We tried to run, but were often held back. When we would have gone forth to do the work of God, we were constrained to turn aside and go alone so that, in weeping and pleading, we might relieve our heavy hearts. We may at times seem to escape from the sorrow, and in the fire of zeal, almost forget its bitterness; yet it returns to us in full strength, and we feel as if a chain were on our limbs. Certainly there is not the bondage arising from any uncertainty as to the relationship in which we stand toward God. These chains fell from us when we received God's record of forgiving love and experienced what it meant to be freely pardoned. No amount of trial can put these chains back on us *if we hold fast the beginning of our assurance firm until the end* (Hebrews 3:14). It is often in a day of grief that we realize most blessedly how completely grace has set us free. Although the chains are not replaced, and we do not again taste the bitterness of bondage, chastisement still is not *joyful, but sorrowful* (Hebrews 12:11); and being sorrowful, it sometimes disheartens and disables us so that we cannot do the same amount of service, or undergo the same degree of work for God, as otherwise we might have done. This is always felt at the first touch of the stroke, for we are men in the flesh, and the flesh gives way. *The spirit is willing, but the flesh is weak* (Matthew 26:41). This continues to be experienced for a considerable time – shorter or longer, according to our natural characters, or according to the elements of the trial.

This is why affliction is often more a season of preparation for service than a time of actual service, except only as patience is service, for, as John Milton wrote, "they also serve who only stand and wait." Let us not be anxious, then, nor cast down because we feel incapacitated for zealous service for a time. Let it be sufficient for us to know that we are preparing for this. Then, when the load is lifted off or becomes lighter, we run with more speed and we labor with more strength and a freer heart. We cannot expect to be wholly free from sorrow here, for some amount of trial is always needed to keep us from forgetting that this is not our rest – that this is the night and not the day; but still, these intervals of calm and sunshine are precious times. They are times of blessing, times of service, and times for the swift race and the busy life.

Affliction is often a season of preparation for service.

These mornings here, coming after the thick nights that gather over us, are most profitable. They not only relieve the "o'er-fraught heart,"[6] but are seasons in which we find leisure to learn lessons of wisdom and holiness, which in the time of the sorrow we had overlooked or put aside from us. The returning elasticity of spirit enables us to rise from our depression now that the weight has in some measure been lifted off.

---

6   This is a phrase from William Shakespeare's play *Macbeth*.

Too continuous a pressure of grief tends to make us moody, selfish, despondent, and slothful. It narrows the circle both of vision and of sympathy, and dries up the springs of our nature. However, when peace returns after a season of trouble, we seem twice as ready as well as strengthened for duty. The trial has made us more serious and has matured us. It has taught us to endure hardness as good soldiers of Jesus Christ (2 Timothy 2:3). It has rubbed off blemishes and has made us less selfish, less contracted in soul. It has taught us to look around with sympathy upon a suffering world and a weeping church. It was as if we had been taken aside for a season into some quiet corner or dark cave from which, while alone and undistracted, we could look out unobserved upon the multitudes that passed and repassed. Then, having been brought in this way to form truer, riper judgments, we are led forth again to act – to act more unselfishly and more zealously, yet more steadfastly and solemnly.

After a night of trial has passed over us, our life should be a life of truer aims, of steadier walk, of higher level, and of sharper, purer vision. If not, we have suffered in vain.

During the night, much was necessarily hidden from us, but the morning reveals what the night had hidden. It shows us how desperate the struggle was between us and our God, of which at the time we were hardly aware. It shows the amount of patience, love, and faithfulness that have been expended on us by God. It shows the extent of the evil in us that had brought down the chastening upon us. It puts us in a position to bring into practice the knowledge of the world's vanity and wretchedness that sorrow had taught us. Consequently, the morning carries out the lessons of the night and gives us opportunity to demonstrate them. Therefore, the alternation of trial and rest that makes up our lot on earth is in truth just a succession of lessons and of opportunities to practice them. *Day to day pours forth speech, and night to night reveals knowledge* (Psalm 19:2).

We see that trial prepares for service. It strengthens us and braces us for toil. It shows us what alone is worth living for so that when the force of it is in some measure diminished, we find ourselves ready to start out again for the race, ready to wield the weapons of our warfare with a firmer and more skillful hand.

These intervals of brightness, then, are the true seasons for labor. These foretastes of the morning should be treasured as opportunities especially provided to us by God for strenuous labor. If spent in this way, how blessed will they be found! They are brief, for tribulation, not ease, is our lot on earth; but this should only stir us up to new vigor, for if they are so brief, we have no time to idle away.

However, it is here that so many people stumble. In trial, they call upon the Lord and vow their life to Him. They say that through evil report and good they will follow Him. On the rough way or the smooth they will walk with Him. By labor, by sacrifice, by watchfulness, and by costly gifts they will prove their love, zeal, and faithfulness! These are good words and sincerely spoken – but so were the words of the disciple: *Even if I have to die with You, I will not deny You* (Matthew 26:35). He spoke what he truly felt, but when the hour came, the courage was not to be found. It is the same with us. Trial calls forth many high thoughts and promptings to noble purposes – yet how seldom do these thoughts ripen; how often do these purposes die! Peace returns, sunshine brightens over us, our broken strength heals again, and we sink back into sloth! The calm hour for which we longed so that we might do something for God has come, but it finds us nearly as careless and selfish as before we entered into the storm.

This must not be. Why were we smitten except that we might be stirred up? Why were we delivered except that we might work more strenuously and more skillfully? How sad, then, that both the trial and the growth would fail of their purposed end!

These times of growth are times of light and gladness. In these mornings, joy has come to us. It is not the mere reaction from sorrow. It is not mere familiarity with suffering. It is not oblivion of the past. It is not the calm of expended feeling. It is joy from the Lord, and the joy of the Lord is our strength (Nehemiah 8:10). He who gave us the night has also given us the morning. He who called up the storm has brought back the calm. It is His joy in which we rejoice, and this joy is our strength. Do not let this strength lie dormant. The calm will not last. The clouds will soon return, and it is good for us to spend well the brief hour of light. *We must work the works of Him who sent Me as long as it is day; night is coming when no one can work* (John 9:4).

Chapter 5

The Morning Star

It was *early morning, while it was still dark* (Mark 1:35), when Jesus rose from the dead. Not the sun, but only the morning star shone upon His opening tomb. The shadows had not fled. The citizens of Jerusalem had not awoken. It was still night – the hour of sleep and of darkness – when He arose. His rising did not break the sleep of the city.

So it will be very early in the morning, when it is still dark, and when nothing but the morning star is shining, that Christ's body, the church, will arise. Like Him, His saints will awake when the children of the night and darkness are still sleeping their sleep of death. In their arising, they disturb no one. The world does not hear the voice that calls them, or if it hears, it will only say that it is thunder, as the unbelieving Jews did when the Father's voice responded to the prayer of Jesus (John 12:29). As Jesus laid them quietly to rest, each in his own still tomb, like children in the arms of their mother, just as quietly and as gently He will awake them when the hour arrives.

He is the Morning Star. *I am the root and the descendant of David, the bright morning star* (Revelation 22:16). This name is given to Him not only because of the glory of His person and the brightness of His appearing, but because of the time when He is to appear.

The first act at His appearing when He comes in glory, the first indication of His arrival, while still in the air, is compared to the shining of the morning star. Afterward He will come forth as *the sun of righteousness* (Malachi 4:2), filling the whole earth with His brightness and shadowing the nations with His healing wings. First, though, He shows Himself as the Morning Star – big with the hope of day, yet not the day; brighter than other stars and eclipsing all of them, yet not the daystar; forerunner of the sun, yet not the sun; foreteller of the dawn, yet not the dawn.

He is the Morning Star.

This is why His promise to the conqueror is, *I will give him the morning star* (Revelation 2:28); that is, I will give Myself to him as the morning star. I will show Myself to him as such. I will confer on him this distinction, this special blessedness.

We read in the Bible of *the eyelids of the morning* (Job 41:18), and the morning star is the first beam shooting from under these lids as they begin to reopen so that the eye of day may again illuminate the earth. It is only those who awake early who see the first opening of these eyelids, gaze upon the morning star, breathe the morning freshness, and taste the morning dew. So it is with those of whom it is said, *Blessed and holy is the one who has a part in the first resurrection* (Revelation 20:6). To them come the inspiring words, *You who lie in the dust, awake and shout for joy* (Isaiah 26:19). The earliest ray of glory finds its way into their tomb. They embrace the first gleams of morning while the eastern clouds still only give the faintest signs of its rising. Its pleasant fragrance, its soothing stillness, its bracing freshness, its sweet loneliness, and its quiet purity – all so solemn and yet so full of hope – these are theirs. Oh, the contrast between these things and the dark night through which they have passed! Oh, the contrast between these things and the grave from which they have arisen! As they shake off the encumbering soil, flinging mortality aside and rising in glorified bodies to meet their Lord in the air, they are illuminated and guided upward, along the primitive pathway, by the beams of that Morning Star, which, like the star of Bethlehem, conducts them to the presence of the King.

There seem to be more periods than one (if times so very brief may be called by that name) opening out upon us when the Lord comes. Just as there are more scenes than one, and more acts than one in the day of the Lord, so there are more periods than one – and it is interesting to notice these in connection with the Morning Star.

All the time up to the moment of His appearing is considered night. Then the scenes change, and step by step, the day with its full sunshine is brought in. First, there is the period of the Morning Star, during which the dead saints awake and the living saints are changed. Then that which is sown in corruption is raised in incorruption, that which is sown in dishonor is raised in glory, that which is sown in weakness is raised in power, and that which is sown a natural body is raised a spiritual body (1 Corinthians 15). Then those who have long dwelt in dust awake and sing. In every land they have found a grave, and every land now gives up the sleeping clay. They come forth *in holy array, from the womb of the dawn* (Psalm 110:3), like the ten thousand times ten thousand dewdrops of the night that are made visible by the morning star and sparkle to its far-coming glory. It has been a long while since light was *sown like seed for the righteous* (Psalm 97:11), and this is the firstfruits of the harvest.

Next there is the period of the twilight. This is the time when *there will be no light; the luminaries will dwindle* (Zechariah 14:6) *as the dawn is spread over the mountains* (Joel 2:2). Then has the last strife of battle begun. Then the Lord with His rod of iron is breaking His enemies in pieces like a potter's vessel (Psalm 2:9). Then He comes forth *from His place to punish the inhabitants of the earth for their iniquity* (Isaiah 26:21). Then, with all His saints, He executes the infinite vengeance, delivers Israel, destroys Antichrist, and lays waste the world with fierce tribulation and purging fire. *Before morning they are no more*, said the prophet, foretelling the ruin of the great enemy of Israel and the church (Isaiah 17:14).

Next there is the morning. The enemy has disappeared; each disaster that marked either his dominion or his destruction is gone. The face of the earth is renewed, the storm is laid to rest, and the glory of an unclouded sun and a clear firmament makes creation sing for joy. The voice of the Beloved is heard:

> *Arise, my darling, my beautiful one, and come along. For behold, the winter is past, the rain is over and gone. The flowers have already appeared in the land; the time has arrived for pruning the vines, and the voice of the turtledove has been heard in our land. The fig tree has ripened its figs, and the vines in blossom have given forth their fragrance. Arise, my darling, my beautiful one, and come along!*
> (Song of Solomon 2:10-13)

Lastly, there is the day in its full brightness. For the path of this Just One is *like the light of dawn, that shines brighter and brighter until the full day* (Proverbs 4:18). Earth has never seen any day like that day. It waits for that day in patient hope, struggling hard, meanwhile, with darkness, and laboring to throw off its long sad weight of affliction.

It is as if the glory of the Lord, when first coming within sight of the earth, showed itself in the far distance as the star of morning. It is a most welcome and hopeful sign, recognized at once by those who knew the true Light of the World (John 8:12), and who had often in other days looked out longingly for the Star of Jacob (Numbers 24:17).

Next, it is as if the same glory, when it neared the earth, showed itself in dreadful majesty as the sign of the Son of Man, which all the tribes of the earth will mourn when they see (Matthew 24:30; Revelation 1:7). Just as in *the morning watch, the LORD looked down on the army of the Egyptians through the pillar of fire and cloud and brought the army of the Egyptians into confusion* (Exodus 14:24), so when He comes with the clouds, *all the tribes of the earth will mourn over Him* (Revelation 1:7).

Next, it is as if the same glory of the Son of Man, coming still nearer, took up its destined position and spread its garments over earth as the pillar of cloud did over the tents of Israel.

Lastly, it is as if this glory, more than shekinah splendor, showed itself as the Sun of Righteousness, bearing healing in His wings with which He heals the nations (Malachi 4:2), so that the inhabitant will no more say, *"I am sick"* (Isaiah 33:24); with which He heals the earth, so that the curse takes flight; and with which He heals the air, so that it poisons no more. Then day to day will pour forth speech in a way unheard of before (Psalm 19:2). Then will their line go out *through all the earth, and their utterances to the end of the world* (Psalm 19:4), when out of that tent that He has placed for the sun, that Sun will come forth as a bridegroom out of his chamber, rejoicing as a strong man to run a race (Psalm 19:4-5). Then will come to pass the saying that is written, *Behold, the glory of the God of Israel was coming from the way of the east. And His voice was like the sound of many waters; and the earth shone with His glory* (Ezekiel 43:2).

The saints are involved in all of these in succession, from the time that they are awakened out of their tombs by the first beams of the Morning Star, to have part in the first resurrection. But it is only the first of these that we are now considering.

The promise to him who overcomes is: *I will give him the morning star* (Revelation 2:28). He is made a partaker of all the blessings symbolized or indicated by that star. The first streak of dawn is his. He is summoned from the dust to meet the morning before even one of its rays has touched the earth. His eye will see the first glimpse of the long-waited-for glory when other eyes still abide in darkness. His soul will rejoice in this first sign of a coming Lord. At the first sound of the returning Bridegroom's voice, he will go forth with ready love. The first object that will meet his eye on awaking from the tomb will be the Star of Jacob.

His soul will rejoice in this first sign of a coming Lord.

This pledge of creation's better day is the portion of the saints. The deliverance of creation is at hand. The time of *the revealing of the sons of God* is come (Romans 8:19). Now clothed in light, themselves the sons of light, they will shine as the brightness of the firmament and as the stars forever and ever (Daniel 12:3). Now transformed into the image of the Morning Star, themselves the stars of morning, they prepare to sing together over the new creation, when its foundations will be fastened and its cornerstone laid by Him who is to make all things new (see Job 38:6-7, which refers to the old creation). Death is now *swallowed up in victory* (1 Corinthians 15:54). The grave is robbed. The spoiler is spoiled. Ashes are exchanged for beauty. The light that was quenched is rekindled. The sorrow passes into joy. The darkness of a brief night ends in the ascendance of the endless day.

As for those *who are alive and remain unto the coming of the Lord* (1 Thessalonians 4:15), even though they will not go before those who are asleep, yet they will not be behind them in the blessedness. They will have the same privileges of the early morning. They will have the same honor and the same glory. Their eye will look upon that Star, and it will be to them all that it is to those who were *lying in the dust* (Isaiah 26:19). Living in the last days of a God-denying world – days as dark and hateful as those of Noah or of Lot – their righteous souls tormented from day to day (2 Peter 2:8) with wickedness that cannot rest (Proverbs 4:16), casting up its mire and dirt on every side (Isaiah 57:20) with danger pressing, conflict thickening, persecution assailing, and sorrows multiplying – how welcome will that sign be to them, springing up like hope when all is hopeless, and promising life, refreshment, rest, and gladness to the troubled and despairing earth!

Like the anxious watchman on some fortress, they have been wearily waiting for the morning, and it has come at last! Like the weary traveler, pressing on over hill and moor and rock and field and thicket, they have been seeking at every turn to catch the light of their cottage window, and it is seen at last! Like the tempest-tossed apostle, when neither sun nor stars appeared for many days (Acts 27:20), they long for the day, and they are glad beyond measure at the signs of its approach. The glimmer of the lighthouse has been their comfort and their guide in the past. They have shaped their way and cheered their hearts by it. But all of a sudden, the beacon seems to sink away, and before they are aware, its light is lost amid the far-surpassing brightness of the Morning Star.

However, that Star rises with no ray of blessing upon the unready and unwatching world. It rises only to shed disastrous torment and give token of the desolations that are at hand. For just as the flood burst forth when Noah entered the ark, or as the fire came down when Lot entered Zoar, so the wrath is poured out and the door is shut when the saints are then caught up in the air.

Until then, the gate of peace stands wide open, and all people are asked to enter the place of safety. The most unready of all the children of men may go freely in, for the grace that invites makes no exceptions, but welcomes the most unworthy. It would gladly attract the seekers of empty joy away from joys that are so vain. It would eagerly win the heart of the sorrowful who mourn and yet have no comforter because they have no God. It would willingly bring those who think they are secure into a place of true safety before the storm arises that is to break in pieces the strong foundations of the earth.

Children of the earth – you especially whose sorrows are multiplied and whose hearts are sick with disappointment – listen to the gracious warning! Enter the hiding place and be safe forever. Thrice blessed are those griefs and disappointments that lead you out of deceptive shelter and into the sure refuge from the storm, that call you from the joy of the world and into the joy of the Lord.

Chapter 6

The Morning

*T*he watchman says, *"Morning comes"* (Isaiah 21:12); and although he forewarns us of night while making this answer, he also assures us of morning. He says that there is a morning, and therefore we should not give in to weakness of spirit. However, there is a night in between; therefore take warning so that you will not be surprised nor dismayed, as if the promise were broken or some strange thing were permitted to happen to you.

There may be delay, he indicates, before the morning – a dark delay for which we should be prepared. He calls us to watchfulness during this time, for the length of the night is hidden and the time of daybreak is left uncertain. We must always be looking, with our eyes focused on the eastern hills. We have nothing with which to measure the hours except for the sorrows of the church and the failing of hearts.

During this delay, the watchman encourages us to

inquire, to return, to come back. He expects us to ask, "How long?" and "When will the night be over?" He takes for granted that this will be the action of people who really long for morning. They will return again and again to the hills of Seir to learn from the watchman what the promise of day is, for no familiarity with the night can ever reconcile them to its darkness or make morning less desirable and welcome.

It is right for us to desire the morning, to hope for it, to long for it, and to inquire as to the signs of it hour after hour. God has set this joy before us, and it would be strange indeed if, when compassed about with so many sorrows, we could forget it or be unconcerned as to its arrival. The coming of the morning is the coming of Him whom we long to see. It is the coming of Him who *changes deep darkness into morning* (Amos 5:8). It is the return of Him whose absence has been night and whose presence will be day. It is the return of Him who is the resurrection and the life (John 11:25), and who brings resurrection with Him. His return is the return of Him who is creation's Lord, and who brings with Him deliverance to creation. It is the return of Him who is the church's Head, and who brings with Him triumph and gladness to His church.

It is right for us to desire the morning.

All the joy, the calm, and the rejuvenating freshness of the morning are wrapped up in Him. When He appears, day appears, life appears, and fruitfulness appears. The curse departs. The *slavery to corruption* is no more (Romans 8:21). Clouds, storms, troubles, and sorrows vanish. The face of nature reassumes the smile of unfallen times. It is earth's festival, the world's jubilee.

> *Let the heavens be glad, and let the earth*
> *rejoice; let the sea roar, and all it contains;*
> *let the field exult, and all that is in it. Then*
> *all the trees of the forest will sing for joy*
> *before the* LORD, *for He is coming, for He is*
> *coming to judge the earth. He will judge the*
> *world in righteousness and the peoples in*
> *His faithfulness.* (Psalm 96:11-13)

This morning has been long anticipated. Age after age it has attracted the church's eye and fixed her hope. Her faith has been resting on the promise of it, and her prayers have gone forth toward the hastening of it. Though afar off, it has been seen, and it has been rejoiced in as the certain end toward which all things are moving forward according to the Father's purpose. "There is a morning" has been the word of consolation brought home to the burdened heart of many saints when they have been ready to say with David, "I am desolate" (Psalm 25:16), or with Jeremiah, *In dark places He has made me dwell, like those who have long been dead* (Lamentations 3:6). Let us dwell for a little on some of these Old Testament allusions to the morning.

Let us look first at Psalm 30. David had been in sorrow, and in coming out of it he makes his consolations known to the saints: *Sing praise to the* LORD, *you His godly ones, and give thanks to His holy name. For His anger is but for a moment, His favor is for a lifetime;*

weeping may last for the night, but a shout of joy comes in the morning (Psalm 30:4-5). He had already tasted the promise of that morning, but he anticipates the morning itself. Then joy has come. Then he can say, *You have turned for me my mourning into dancing; You have loosed my sackcloth and girded me with gladness* (Psalm 30:11).

However, it is a greater voice than David's that is heard in this psalm. This is one of Christ's resurrection psalms, like the 18th and the 116th. He was lifted up so that His enemies were not made to rejoice over Him (Psalm 30:1). He cried out and was healed (Psalm 30:2). His soul was brought up from the grave (Psalm 30:3). There was anger against Him *for a moment*, when He bore the sinner's curse as the sinner's substitute, but in Jehovah's favor there was life (Psalm 30:5). He had a night of weeping, a night of *loud crying and tears* (Hebrews 5:7), when His soul was sorrowful *to the point of death* (Matthew 26:38), and when beneath the waves of that sorrow He sunk, committing His spirit into His Father's hands (Luke 23:46). But it was a night no more. Morning came, and with morning came joy (Psalm 30:5). Coming forth from the tomb, He left all His sorrow behind. His sackcloth was put aside, and He arose clothed with gladness (Psalm 30:11). He found morning and joy, and He is *the first fruits of those who are asleep* (1 Corinthians 15:20). His rising was the rising of His saints. There was a morning for Him; therefore, there will be one for us – a morning bright with resurrection glory.

Let us look next at Psalm 49. These are Christ's words,

as is proved by Matthew 13:35, which quotes verse 4. He summons the whole world to listen. He speaks of wisdom (Psalm 49:3), for He is Wisdom. He points to the vanity of riches and their insufficiency to redeem a soul (Psalm 49:6-7), and who knew as well as He what a ransom was needed? He sees people continuing in their wickedness, self-confidence, and pride. He proclaims their absurdity and guilt – speaking of them

Victory in the morning is that to which we look forward.

as incurable from generation to generation. He contrasts the end of the wicked and the end of the righteous; *as sheep they are appointed for Sheol* (Psalm 49:14), buried out of sight, forgotten and unmourned. *The upright shall rule over them in the morning* (Psalm 49:14). The morning then brings dominion to the righteous – redemption from the power of the grave.

Jesus rejoiced in this; let us rejoice in this also. This joy of the morning was set before Him (Hebrews 12:2); it is the same joy that is set before us. Victory in the morning is that to which we look forward – a share in the first resurrection, of which those who are partakers live and reign with Christ (Revelation 20:6).

Now look at the forty-sixth Psalm. It is the statement of the faith of Israel's faithful ones in the time of Jacob's trouble (Jeremiah 30:7). The earth is shaken (Psalm 46:2; see also Haggai 2:6 and Hebrews 12:26-27) and the sea and the waves roar (Psalm 46:3; see also Luke 21:25), but there is a river whose streams make them glad (Psalm 46:4). God is in the midst of her, she will not be moved; God will help her when morning dawns

(Psalm 46:5), just *as in the morning watch* He looked out from the fiery cloud and troubled the Egyptians (Exodus 14:24). Then the heathen are scattered at His voice, He sweeps away every enemy, He makes wars to cease, and He sets Himself on high over the nations as King of kings, exalted in the earth (Psalm 46:10). We see from this that the morning brings with it deliverance from danger, victory over enemies, the renewal of the earth, peace to the nations, and the establishment of Messiah's glorious throne. What a morning of joy that must be for the church, for Israel, and for the whole earth – resurrection for the church, restoration for Israel, and restitution for the earth!

Look at Psalm 110. We see Jesus at Jehovah's right hand, waiting until His enemies are made His footstool (Psalm 110:1). Then He who said unto Him, *Sit* will say, *Arise* (Psalm 82:8). He is yet to have dominion on earth and to sit upon the throne of His father David. Instead of *a disobedient and obstinate people* (Isaiah 65:2; Romans 10:21) as He had in the day of His weakness, He is to have people who *volunteer freely* in the day of His power, in holy array, more numerous and resplendent than the dew *from the womb of the dawn* (Psalm 110:3). Willingness, beauty, holiness, brightness, and number will mark His people in that morning of joy that His coming will produce. Edward Irving wrote in his *Exposition of the Book of Revelation*:

The dew is deposited in greatest plenty about the breaking of the dawn, and refreshes with its numerous drops the leaves and plants and blades of grass on which it rests; so shall the saints of God, coming forth from their invisible abodes out of the womb of the morning, refresh the world with their kind influence; and therefore they are compared to the dew, for all nature is so constituted of God as to bear witness of that day of regeneration that will then dawn.

Read also *the last words of David* (2 Samuel 23:1), in which, as in Psalm 72, *He who rules over men righteously, who rules in the fear of God, is as the light of the morning when the sun rises, a morning without clouds, when the tender grass springs out of the earth, through sunshine after rain* (2 Samuel 23:3-4). Not until the Just One comes is the morning to dawn, for He is its light, and from His countenance is to break forth that light in which all earth is to rejoice. Then the darkness of the long night will disappear, and the brief tribulation tasted in the time of absence will be forgotten in the abundant blessedness of His everlasting presence.

Let us hear how, in the Song of Solomon, the bride refers to this same morning. She rejoices in the Bridegroom's assured love, and her desires or longings are not doubts as to the relationship in which she stands to Him. This is a settled thing with her, for she has tasted that the Lord is gracious. *I am my beloved's and my beloved is mine* (Song of Solomon 6:3). What direction then do her longings take? Her eyes are toward the hills, over which she expects to see Him coming like a roe (Song of Solomon 2:8). Thus she pleads with Him not to delay: *Hurry, my beloved, and be like a gazelle or a young stag on the mountains of spices* (Song of Solomon 8:14).

Thus also she anticipates the morning of fuller joy,

even while enjoying present fellowship: *He pastures his flock among the lilies. Until the cool of the day when the shadows flee away, turn, my beloved, and be like a gazelle or a young stag on the mountains of Bether* (Song of Solomon 2:16-17). Thus the Bridegroom Himself, feeling, if one may so speak, the loneliness of the night and that it is not good to be alone, longs for day, like His bride, and resolves

Let us meet Him on that hill in faith.

to climb the hills where He may not only be delighted with freshest scents, but may catch the earliest gleam of dawn: *Until the cool of the day when the shadows flee away, I will go my way to the mountain of myrrh and to the hill of frankincense* (Song of Solomon 4:6). Let us meet Him on that hill in faith, and watch with Him in hope, yet always remembering that although this joy that faith gives here is unspeakably comforting, it is not the gladness of the marriage supper. It is not the blessedness of the wedding day. For He Himself, while telling His disciples, *Lo, I am with you always* (Matthew 28:20), also said, *I will not drink of this fruit of the vine from now on until that day when I drink it new with you in My Father's kingdom* (Matthew 26:29).

Thus we see all kinds of joy brought within the circle of this morning. It is a morning of joy because it is the morning introduced by Him who said, *These things I have spoken to you so that My joy may be in you, and that your joy may be made full* (John 15:11). It is the morning introduced by Him of whom we can say, *In Your presence is fullness of joy; in Your right hand there are pleasures forever* (Psalm 16:11). Let us now look at the different kinds of joy and the different illustrations signifying it.

There is the joy of deliverance from overwhelming danger. This was the joy of the Jews when their adversary perished and Mordecai was exalted: *For the Jews there was light and gladness and joy and honor. . . . There was gladness and joy for the Jews, a feast and a holiday* (Esther 8:16-17). This is how the church's joy will be in the morning of her great deliverance.

There is the joy of escape from captivity and return from exile, such as that which made Israel feel *like those who dream* (Psalm 126:1). Such will be the church's joy when her long captivity is over. Then her mouth will be filled with laughter, and her tongue with singing (Psalm 126:2). *Those who sow in tears shall reap with joyful shouting* (Psalm 126:5).

There is the joy of harvest (Isaiah 9:3), and this will be the church's joy.

There is the mother's joy when her pangs are over and the child is born into the world (John 16:21). We will rejoice with such joy, and no one can take our joy from us. The joy in reserve for us is diverse and large. It will remain and satisfy. It is the joy of the morning. A long, glad day is before us. There will be no evening with its lengthening shadows, and no night with its chills and darkness. *There will no longer be any night; and they will not have need of the light of a lamp nor the light of the sun, because the Lord God will illumine them; and they will reign forever and ever* (Revelation 22:5).

The prospect of this morning – this morning of joy – strengthens and encourages us under all our tribulation. If this morning were an uncertainty, how dark would the night seem! How difficult it would be for us to fight against weakness and despair! However, the thought of morning invigorates and strengthens us. We can set our faces to the storm, for behind it lies the calm. We can bear the parting, for the meeting is not far away. We can afford to weep, for the tears will soon be wiped away. We can watch the tedious sickbed, for soon *no resident will say, "I am sick"* (Isaiah 33:24). We can look quietly into the grave of buried love and cherished hope, for resurrection shines beyond it. Things may be against us here, but they are for us hereafter. The here is only an hour, but the hereafter is a whole eternity.

However, for the world – the neglectful, pleasure-chasing world, they have no such light for their dark hours of sorrow. No morning comes to them. Their sun sets, but does not rise again. Their life goes down in darkness without a hope. It is night – infinite and endless night to them – the blackness of darkness forever (Jude 1:13)! There is no healing of their wounds, no wiping away of their tears, and no bandaging of their broken hearts! They reject the infinite sacrifice, they waste away their day of salvation in amusement, and their history winds up in judgment and the second death. *If they do not speak according to this word, it is because they have no dawn* (Isaiah 8:20). They reject or ridicule this word that was preached to them by the gospel (1 Peter 1:25), and vengeance overtakes them for rejection! *Evil will come on you which you will not know how to charm away; and disaster will fall on you for which you cannot atone; and destruction about which*

you do not know will come on you suddenly (Isaiah 47:11).
Their portion is an evil without deliverance and a night
without a morning!

That is a sad end of a lifetime of weariness! They
have never known joy, even though its full cup has often
been handed to them by God, and they were urged to
drink it! Each message, each appeal, and each warning is simply God saying to them, "Come and share
My love! Come and taste My joy!" They have known
sorrow, for how could they miss knowing it in such a
world? Heavy burdens, intense griefs, sharp stings, bitter memories, difficult doubts, intolerable forebodings,
and dark self-questionings: "What am I, or what will
I be?" All these, crowding in upon a soul that has no
God, and pouring into a heart that has no outlet for its
sorrows in the arms of a Savior, are enough to dry up
life's springs, even when deepest. Yet all these are only
the beginning of sorrows! There is a fuller cup yet to be
given to them to drink: eternal wormwood! The heart
would gladly break then, but cannot, for the sorrow is
as eternal as it is infinite. They will seek for death, but
will not be able to find it – for the second death is the
death that never dies.

Johann Wolfgang von Goethe, the world's favor-
ite, if one may so speak, confessed when he was about
eighty years old that he could not remember being in
a really happy state of mind even for a few weeks at a
time, and that when he wanted to feel comfortable, he
had to hide his self-consciousness! The following is the
closing section of his autobiography:

Child, child, no more! The coursers of time, lashed

as it were, by invisible spirits, hurry in the light car of our destiny; and all that we can do, is in cool self-possession to hold the reins with a firm hand, and to guide the wheels, now to the left, now to the right, a stone here, a precipice there. Whither it is hurrying who can tell? And who indeed can remember the point from which it started?

How sad it is for the poor world that with all its refinement and poetry and philosophy, it does not know where it is hurrying! It is as if no voice (more than man's) had ever said, *I am the way, and the truth, and the life* (John 14:6).

Chapter 7

The Victory over Death

The issue of the conflict between the saints and death was decided when the Lord arose. He met the enemy on his own territory, his own battlefield, and overcame. He entered the palace of the king of terrors, and there laid hold of the strong man, shaking his dwelling to its foundations as he came forth, carrying away its gates along with Him, and giving warning of being about to return in order to complete His conquest by seizing his goods and taking from him the treasures that he had kept so long – the dust of sleeping saints.

The first act of seizing the strong man's goods began at the resurrection. We have already spoken about this generally, but the subject is so much dwelt upon in Scripture that something more specific is needed. It is a hope so fruitful in consolation to us who are still sojourners in a dying world like this, yet so little prized, that we must not carelessly pass it by. Let us look at it in the aspects in which the apostle Paul spreads it out before us in 1 Corinthians 15.

The vision that he holds there before us is one of glory and joy. It is a morning landscape, and it contrasts brightly with present night and sorrow. It draws aside the veil that hides our much-longed-for heritage from view, showing us from our vantage point the excellence of the land that will so soon be ours – plains richer than Sharon, valleys more fruitful than Sibmah, and mountains mightier than Carmel or Lebanon. The then and the now, the there and the here, are strangely diverse. Here is the mortal, there the immortal; here is the corruptible, there the incorruptible; here the earthly, there the heavenly; here the dominion of death, there death swallowed up in victory; here the grave devouring its prey, there the spoiler of the grave coming forth in resurrection power to claim each particle of holy dust, undoing death's handiwork, spoiling the spoiler, bringing forth in beauty that which had been laid down in vileness, and clothing with honor that which had been sown in shame.

The trumpet will sound, and the dead will be raised imperishable, and we will be changed. All this will happen *in a moment, in the twinkling of an eye* (1 Corinthians 15:52). Other changes are gradual, but this one is sudden. There is the ebbing and the flowing. There is the growing up into manhood, and the growing down into old age. There is the slow opening of spring into summer, and of summer into autumn. However, this will be unlike all these changes. It will be instantaneous, like the lightning's flash or the twinkling of an eye. He who spoke and it was done will speak again, and it will be done. He who said, *"Let there be light"; and there was light* (Genesis 1:3) will speak, and light will come forth out of the grave's thick darkness.

This perishable must put on the imperishable (1 Corinthians 15:53)! There will be an entire casting aside of mortality with all its wrappings of corruption and all its remains of dishonor. Every particle of evil will be shaken out of us, and this vile body will be transfigured into the likeness of the Lord's own glorious body (Philippians 3:21). We entered this world mortal and corruptible, and all our life long we are soaking up mortality and corruption, becoming more and more thoroughly mortal and corruptible. The grave sets its seal to all this, and crumbles us down into common earth. But the trumpet sounds, and all this is gone. Mortality falls off, and everything connected with it is left behind. No more impurity or disease remains in us. We can then defy sickness, pain, and death. We can say to our bodies, "Have pain no more"; to our limbs, "Be weary no more"; to our lips, "Be thirsty no more"; and to our eye, "Be dim no more."

The trumpet sounds, and all this is gone.

O death, where is your sting? (1 Corinthians 15:55). He who has the power of death is the devil, the old serpent, and he torments us here. Sin gave him his sting, and the law gave sin its strength – but now that sin has been forgiven and the law magnified, the sting is removed. The stinging begins with our birth, and life throughout is one unending battle with death until, for a season, death conquers and we fall beneath his power. However, the prey will be taken from the mighty, and his victims will be rescued forever. Now sin has passed away, and what has become of death's sting – its sharpness, its pain, and its power to kill? It cannot touch the immortal and the incorruptible!

O death, where is your victory? (1 Corinthians 15:55). Grave, you have been a conqueror all along, never yet defeated. Your career has been one perpetual triumph. You have been the ally of death, following in his footsteps. You not only smite down the victim, but you devour it, taking it into your den, and consuming it bone by bone until every particle is crumbled into dust, as if to make victory so certain that retrieving it would be absolutely impossible. Yet your victories are over. The tide of battle is turned in the twinkling of an eye. Look at these rising multitudes. You cannot hold them any longer. You thought they were your prey, but they were only given to you to keep for a little moment.

See these holy ones, without one spot, not one stain on which your sting, O death, can fasten. There is not a weakness that might encourage you again to hope for a second victory! All your work of six thousand years has been undone in a moment! Not a scar remains from all your many wounds. There is not a trace, disfigurement, or blemish. It is all perfection – eternal beauty! Look at these other holy ones, also glorified! They have not tasted death nor entered into the grave. You have had no power over them. You have waged war with them in vain. They have seen no corruption, and they remain monuments that you were not invincible. They have defied the power, and now they are beyond your reach!

Ah, this is victory! It is not escaping by stealth out of the hands of the enemy, but it is conquering him! It is not bribing him to let us go, but it is open and triumphant victory – victory that not only defeats and disgraces the enemy, but swallows him up. It is victory achieved in righteousness, and in behalf of these who had once been lawful captives (Isaiah 49:24).

And the victor, who is He? Not we, but our Brother-King. His sword smote the mighty one, and under His shield we have become conquerors. The wreath is His, not ours, because of His victorious battle. We are the trophies, not the conquerors. He overcame. How? By allowing Himself to be overcome! He plucked the sting from death. How? By allowing it to pierce Himself! He made the grave release its grip. How? By going down into its precincts and wrestling with it in the greatness of His strength. He brought the law that was against us around to be on our side. How? By giving the law all that it sought so that it could ask no more either of Him or of us.

How complete the victory over us seemed for a while to be, yet how complete the reversal was! These enemies are not only conquered, but more than conquered. No trace of their former conquests remains. We not only live, but are made immortal. We are not only rescued from the corruption of the grave, but we are made incorruptible forever.

Victory, then, is our watchword. We entered on the conflict at first, assured of final victory by Him who said, *I am the resurrection and the life; he who believes in Me will live even if he dies, and everyone who lives and believes in Me will never die* (John 11:25-26); and who to all His many promises of spiritual life and blessing added this: *and I Myself will raise him up on the last day* (John 6:40). When taking up sword and shield, we were sure of success. When putting on the armor, we could boast as he who takes it off in triumph.

Victory was our watchword during every conflict, even the hardest and the severest. Victory was our watchword on the bed of death, in the dark valley, when going down for a season into the tomb. Victory is to be our final watchword when reappearing from the grave, leaving mortality beneath us and ascending to glory.

Then Jehovah God will wipe away every tear from off all faces (Isaiah 25:8; 30:19; 35:10; 60:20; Jeremiah 31:12; Revelation 7:17; 21:4). We will weep no more. The furrows of past tears are gone. Tears of anguish, tears of parting, tears of bereavement, tears of adversity, and tears of heartbreaking sorrow are all forgotten. We *cannot* weep again. The fountain of tears is dried up. God our Lord wipes up the tears. It is not time that heals the sorrows of the saints or dries up their tears, but it is God – God Himself – God alone. He reserves this for Himself as if it were His special joy. The world's only refuge in grief is time or pleasure, but the refuge of the saints is God. This is the true healing of the wound. We have the assurance that tears once wiped away by God cannot flow again.

He will remove the reproach of His people from all the earth (Isaiah 25:8). As He is to do this for Israel, so He will also do this for the church. Rebuke, reproach, and persecution have been the church's portion on earth. The world hated the Master, and they have hated the servant (John 15:18). *The reproach of Christ* (Hebrews 11:26) is a well-known reproach. Shame for His name is what His saints have been enduring, and will continue to endure until He comes again. But all this is to be reversed. Soon the world's ridicule will cease. They will mock no more. They will hate no more. They will revile no more. They will no longer cast out our names as evil. Honor crowns the saints, and their enemies are put to shame. It is only one day's reviling before men, and *Let us be of good cheer.* then there will be an eternity of glory in the presence of God and of the Lamb. Then the name of saint will be a name of glory, both in earth and heaven.

Then why shy away from the world's reproach when it is merely a breath at the most, and when we know that it so soon will cease? Why not rejoice that we are counted worthy to suffer shame for the name of Jesus (Acts 5:41) when we know that all that afflicts us here is not worthy to be compared with the glory that will be revealed in us (Romans 8:18)? The morning, and the glory that the morning brings with it, will more than compensate for it all. Let us be of good cheer then, and press onward, through evil report as well as through good, *looking to the reward* (Hebrews 11:26).

The creation itself also will be set free from its slavery to corruption into the freedom of the glory of the children of God (Romans 8:21). That morning that brings resurrection to us brings restitution to creation. It brings deliverance to a groaning earth. The same Lord that brings us out of the tomb rolls back the curse from off creation, removing the remains of the first Adam's sin and presenting a fresh memorial of the second Adam's righteousness. It will be a happy world when Satan is bound, the curse is obliterated, the bondage is broken, the air is purged, the soil is cleansed, the grave is emptied, and the risen saints take the throne of creation to rule in righteousness with the scepter of the righteous King!

Resurrection is our hope. It is our hope in life and our hope in death. It is a purifying hope. It is a comforting hope. It comforts us when we are laying in the grave the bodies of those whom we have loved. It cheers us when feeling the weakness of our own body and thinking how soon we will lie down in dust. It refreshes and elevates us when we remember how much precious dust earth has received since the day of righteous Abel. How sweet that name of resurrection! It pours life into each vein and strength into each nerve at the very mention of it!

It is not worldly, then, to bend over the clay-cold corpse and long for the time when these very limbs will move again, when that hand will clasp ours as it used to do, when those eyes will brighten, when those lips will resume their suspended utterance, and when we will feel the throbbings of that heart again! No, it is scriptural and it is spiritual. Some may call it senti-mental, but it is our very nature. We cannot feel oth-erwise, even if we want to. We cannot help but love the clay. We cannot do other than to be reluctant to part with it. We cannot help not to desire its reanimation. The nature that God has given us can be satisfied with nothing less, and with nothing less has God determined to satisfy it. *Your brother will rise again* (John 11:23). *God will bring with Him those who have fallen asleep in Jesus* (1 Thessalonians 4:14).

We feel the weight of that mortality that often makes life a burden, yet we say, *We do not want to be unclothed but to be clothed, so that what is mortal will be swallowed up by life* (2 Corinthians 5:4). We lay the desire of our eyes in the grave, yet we cling to the remains, and we feel as if the dirt that struck the coffin were wounding the body on which it falls. At such a moment, the thought of opening graves and rising dust is unutterably precious. We will see that face again. We will hear that voice again. Not only does the soul that filled that clay still live, but that clay itself will be revived. Our risen friend will be in very deed – form, appearance, and voice – the friend whom we have known and loved. Our risen brother will be everything that we knew him to be here when, hand in hand, we passed through the wilderness together, encouraged with the blessed thought that no separation could part us for long, and that the grave itself could unlink neither hands nor hearts.

Chapter 8

The Reunion

The family has been a scattered one all along. Not only has it been scattered along the ages, but it has been dispersed over every land. "Children of the dispersion" might well be the name of its members. They have no continuing city. They have no city at all that they can call their own. They are certain of nothing here beyond their bread and clothing. They are not able to count upon any certain dwelling, yet they always have the promise of it somewhere.

Besides this scattering that occurred as they were called out of every kindred and nation, there are others that are more bitter. There is the scattering caused by persecution when it drives them from city to city. There is the scattering caused by adversity when happy circles are broken up and their fragments are sent far apart. There is the scattering often caused by jealousy and contention and selfish rivalry, even among the saints. There is the scattering caused by bereavement when strong ties are broken and warm love is spilt like water on the ground – when fellowship is torn apart and living relationships are chilled by death, and tears of choking anguish are the only relief of loneliness and sorrow.

As Israel was scattered among the nations, so the saints have been – not indeed like Israel, because of the wrath of God against them, but still scattered everywhere. *The LORD will scatter you among all peoples, from one end of the earth to the other end of the earth* (Deuteronomy 28:64). Those were God's words to Israel, and the church feels how truly they suit her condition as a scattered flock.

In early times, and often since then, in days of trouble and persecution, it was truly and literally a scattering, just as when the autumn wind blows down and tosses the dry leaves to and fro. But in our day, it is not so much a scattering as a simple dwelling asunder, by the calling out of every nation the few that make up the little flock. It is a gathering *out,* but not a gathering *together.* It is one family, yet the members do not know each other and do not see each other in the flesh. They are drawn by the Father's hand and according to the Father's purpose – out of kingdoms and families wide apart. They have no local center of interest, residence, or of government. They have no common home and no common meeting place except that which faith gives them now in their Head above, or that hope assures them of in the world to come, where they will come together, face to face, as one household, gathered under one roof and seated around one table.

This separation and apparent disunion are not natural or congenial, for there is a hidden magnetic virtue that unconsciously and irresistibly draws them toward each other. Separation is the present law of the kingdom, but this is only because election is the law of the dispensation. There is a closeness among the members that neither time nor distance can destroy. There is a love kin-

The saints have not been exempted from griefs.

dled they know not how, and kept alive they know not how, but this love of kin, this love of brotherhood, is strong and unquenchable. "No distance breaks the tie of blood. Brothers are brothers evermore."[7]

And they feel this. Knit by the ties of a strange and unearthly union, they have a conscious feeling of oneness that nothing can shake. Deeply hidden in each other's heart of hearts, they cannot consent to be perpetually apart, but eagerly anticipate the day of promised union.

There is also another kind of separation that they have had to endure. Death has torn them from each other. From Abel downward, there has been one long scene of bereavement. The griefs of parting make up the greatest amount of earthly suffering among the children of men. The saints have not been exempted from these griefs. Bitter have been the farewells that have been spoken on earth – around the deathbed, in the prison, on the seashore, on the home threshold, or in the city of strangers – the farewells of people who

---

7   This is from a poem by John Keble (1792-1866) that begins with "The clouds that wrap the setting sun."

knew that they would meet no more until the grave gave up that which had been committed to its care. Death has been the great scatterer, and the tomb has been the great receiver of the fragments.

Our night of weeping has taken much of its gloom and sadness from these torn relationships. The pain of parting, in the case of the saints, has much to alleviate it, but still the bitterness is there. We feel that we must separate, and although it is only for a while, our hearts still bleed with the wound.

However, there is reunion, and one of the joys of the morning is this reunion among the saints. During the night they had been scattered, but in the morning they are gathered together. In the wilderness they have been separated, but in the kingdom they will meet. During this age they have been like the drops of the occasional shower, but in the age to come they will be like the dew of Hermon – the dew that descended upon the mountains of Zion – one gleaming gathering settling upon the holy hills and bringing refreshment to a weary earth. Then the prayer of the Lord will fully be answered:

> *That they may all be one; even as You,*
> *Father, are in Me and I in You, that they*
> *also may be in Us, so that the world may*
> *believe that You sent Me. The glory which*
> *You have given Me I have given to them,*
> *that they may be one, just as We are one; I*
> *in them and You in Me, that they may be*
> *perfected in unity, so that the world may*

know that You sent Me, and loved them,
even as You have loved Me. (John 17:21-23)

I will strike down the shepherd, and the sheep of the
flock shall be scattered (Matthew 26:31). This is our
present position – a struck-down Shepherd and a scattered flock! However, the day is at hand when He who
scattered will gather (Jeremiah 31:10), and there will
be a glorified Shepherd and a gathered flock. It will not
be merely one flock, one fold, and one Shepherd, but
it will be one flock gathered into one fold around the
one Shepherd. The scattering will cease, the wandering will be at an end, the famine will be exchanged for
the green pastures, the danger will be forgotten, and
the devouring lion will be bound. Then the prophecy
regarding the issues of the Surety's death will fully come
to pass: *that He might also gather together into one the*
children of God who are scattered abroad (John 11:52).
Then what is written of Israel will, in a higher sense,
be fulfilled in the church:

> *Behold, I Myself will search for My sheep*
> *and seek them out. As a shepherd cares for*
> *his herd in the day when he is among his*
> *scattered sheep, so I will care for My sheep*
> *and will deliver them from all the places to*
> *which they were scattered on a cloudy and*
> *gloomy day. . . . I will feed them in a good*
> *pasture, and their grazing ground will be on*
> *the mountain heights of Israel. . . . Then I*
> *will set over them one shepherd, My servant*

David, and he will feed them; he will
feed them himself and be their shepherd.
(Ezekiel 34:11-12, 14, 23)

As the gathering of Israel is to be a blessing diffusing itself on every side, so the reunion of the scattered church is to be to the world. Therefore, we may use Israel's promise here also: *I will make them and the places around My hill a blessing. And I will cause showers to come down in their season; they will be showers of blessing* (Ezekiel 34:11-26).

This reunion is when the Lord returns. When the Head appears, then the members come together. They have always been united, for just as the Godhead was still united to the manhood of Christ, even when His body was in the tomb, so the oneness between the members, both with each other and with their Head, has always been kept unbroken. However, when He comes, this union will be fully felt, realized, seen, and manifested. *When Christ, who is our life, is revealed, then you also will be revealed with Him in glory* (Colossians 3:4).

Our reunion will be in incorruption.

This reunion is at *the resurrection of the righteous* (Luke 14:14). Every remaining particle of separation is then removed. Soul and body meet – both perfect. No trace remains of this vile body or this dust-cleaving soul. The corruptible has gone, and the incorruptible has come. Our reunion will be in incorruption – hands that will never grow arthritic clasping each other, renewing broken companionships, and eyes that will never dim gazing on each other with purer love.

This reunion is in the cloud of glory, in which the Lord comes again. When He went up from the Mount of Olives, this cloud received Him, and His disciples would have gladly gone up along with Him. But into that glorious pavilion – His tabernacle – they will yet ascend. There they will meet with Him, embrace each other, and come together into that mysterious dwelling place, from the four winds of heaven, *from every nation and all tribes and peoples and tongues* (Revelation 7:9).

This reunion is the marriage day, and that cloud-curtained pavilion is the Bridegroom's chamber. There the bride is now seen as one, and there she realizes her own oneness in a way unimagined before. There, too, the marriage feast is spread, and the bride takes her place of honor at the marriage table – *glorious within* (Psalm 45:13), as well as without – not like the harlot-bride, *who was clothed in fine linen and purple and scarlet, and adorned with gold and precious stones and pearls* (Revelation 18:16), but *in fine linen, bright and clean* (Revelation 19:8).

It is to this reunion, and to the honors that will then be given to the whole church at once, that the apostle refers when he says that the Old Testament saints, to whom the promises came, *would not be made perfect* apart from us (Hebrews 11:40). Thus he suggests that the actual possession of the thing promised has not yet been given. It is deferred until the Lord comes so that no age, group, or individuals of the church would be perfectly blest and glorified before the rest, for all must be raised up together, all caught up together, and all crowned together since they are one body, one bride. He points to the day of the Lord as the day of our common introduction into the inheritance; the day of our common reentrance into Eden; the day when, as one vast multitude of all kindreds, we will enter in through the gates into the city; the day of our common crowning and our common triumph. It is to be one crowning, one enthroning, one festival, one triumph, and one entrance for the whole church from the beginning. The members are not crowned alone, nor in segments, nor in groups – but in one glorious hour they receive their everlasting crowns and take their seats, side by side with their Lord and with each other, in simultaneous gladness, upon the long-expected throne.

The preparations for this union have been being made for a long time. They began with us individually, when first the scattered fragments of our souls were brought together by the Holy Spirit at our conversion. Before that, our hearts were divided and faithless (Hosea 10:2), and this was our special sin. But then they were united, at least in some measure, though still calling for the unceasing prayer, *Unite my heart to fear Your name* (Psalm 86:11). First it was the inner man that came under the power of sin and was broken into parts; then the outer man followed. Both were created whole in every sense of that word, and both have ceased to be whole in any sense of it. When restoration begins, it begins with the reunion of the inner man, and it moves on to the outer man in the resurrection, bringing together the two restored parts. It was the individual that was first subjected to sin, and then the multitude. Therefore, it is the individual that is first restored. This is the process that is now going on under the almighty, life-giving, uniting energy of the Holy Spirit. But the reunion is not complete until oneness is brought back to the multitude, to the body, until all those members that have been individually restored are brought together, and so the body is made whole.

It is for this that we wait until the Lord comes. For as it was the first Adam who broke creation into fragments, so it is the second Adam who is to restore creation in all its parts and regions and make it one again. The good and the evil are then parted forever, but the good and the good are brought into perfect oneness – a oneness so complete and so abiding as to more than compensate for brokenness and separation here.

The soul and the body come together and form one glorified man. The ten thousand members of the church come together and form one glorified church. The scattered stones come together and form one living temple. The bride and the Bridegroom meet. *Here* it has been *one Lord, one faith, one baptism* (Ephesians 4:5); *there* it will be one body, one bride, one vine, one temple, one family, one city, and one kingdom.

The broken fruitfulness and the erratic fluctuation of the cursed earth will pass into the unbroken beauty of the new creation. The discord of the troubled elements will be laid, and harmony will return. The warring animals will lie down in peace.

Then heaven and earth will come together into one. That which we call distance is annihilated. The curtain closed by sin is withdrawn from between the upper and the lower glory, and the fields of a paradise that was never lost are brought into a happy neighborhood with the fields of paradise regained. God's purpose develops itself in the oneness of a two-fold glory: the rulers and the ruled, the risen and the unrisen, the celestial and the terrestrial, the glory that is in the heaven above and the glory that is in the earth beneath. *There are also heavenly bodies and earthly bodies, but the glory of the heavenly is one, and the glory of the earthly is another* (1 Corinthians 15:40).

We need to dwell upon such scenes so that as our tribulations abound, so also our consolations may abound (2 Corinthians 1:5). Our wounds here take a long time to heal. Bereavements keep the heart bleeding for a long time. Melancthon, with a tender simplicity so typical of himself, refers to his feelings when his child was taken from him by death. He wept as he recalled the past. It pierced his soul to remember the time when once, as he sat weeping, his little one with its little napkin wiped the tears from his cheeks.

Our wounds here take a long time to heal.

Remembrances like these haunt us through life, occasionally newly brought up by passing scenes. Some summer morning's sun recalls, with stinging freshness, the hour when that same sun streamed in through our window upon a dying infant's cradle, as if to bring out all the beauty of a parting smile and engrave it upon our hearts forever. Or is it a funeral scene that comes to memory – a funeral scene that only a few days earlier had been a wedding scene – and never on earth can we forget the outburst of our grief when we saw the bridal flowers laid upon a newly dug grave. Maybe some wintry noon recalls the time and the scene when we laid a parent's dust within its resting place and left it to sleep in winter's grave of snows. These memories haunt us, pierce us, and make us feel what a desolate place this is, and what an infinitely desirable thing it would be to meet these lost ones again – where the meeting will be eternal.

Consequently, the tidings of this reunion in the many mansions are like greetings from home. They relieve the afflicted heart. They direct us to be of good cheer, for the separation is only brief, and the meeting to which we look forward will be the happiest ever enjoyed. The time of sorrowful remembrances will soon pass, and no remembrance will remain except that which will make our joy overflow.

Everything connected with this reunion is suited to enhance its blessedness. To meet again anywhere, or in any way, or at any time would be blessed; how much more at such a time, in such circumstances, and in such a home! The dark past lies behind us like a prison from which we have come forth, or like a wreck from which we have escaped in safety and landed in a quiet haven. We meet where separation is an impossibility, where distance no more tests devotion, troubles the spirit, or spoils the joy of loving.

We meet in a kingdom. We meet at a marriage table. We meet in the prepared city (Hebrews 11:16), the new Jerusalem (Revelation 21). We meet under the shadow of the Tree of Life and on the banks of the river of life. We meet to celebrate and to sing the songs of triumph. It was joyous to meet here for a day; how much more to meet in the kingdom forever! It was delightful to meet, even with parting fully in view; how much more so when no such cloud hangs over our future! It was satisfying to meet in the wilderness and the land of graves; how much more in paradise and in the land where death does not enter! It was sweet to meet in the night, although it was cold and dark; how much more in the morning, when light has risen, the troubled sky is cleared, and joy is spreading itself around us like a new atmosphere from which every element of sorrow has disappeared!

Chapter 9

The Presence of the Lord

To love in absence, though with the knowledge of being beloved, and with the certainty of meeting before long, is but a mixed joy. It contents us in the place of something better and more blessed, but it lacks that which true love longs for – the presence of the beloved one. That presence fills up the joy and turns every shadow into brightness.

This is especially true when this time of absence is a time of weakness and suffering and enduring wrong; when dangers come abundantly around, enemies spare not, and advantage is taken by the strong to trouble or injure the defenseless. Then love in absence, although felt to be a sure consolation, is found to be insufficient, and the heart comforts itself with the thought that the interval of loneliness is brief and that the days of separation are quickly running out.

It is with such feelings that we look forward to meeting with Him whom having not seen, we love

(1 Peter 1:8), and anticipate the joy of being forever *with the Lord* (1 Thessalonians 4:17). That day of meeting has enough gladness in it to make up for all the past. In addition, it is eternal. It is not meeting today and parting tomorrow, but it is meeting once and forever. How wonderful it would be to see Him face to face even for a day! How much more so to be with Him for a lifetime, or an age, even if there were intervals of absence between! However, to be with Him forever – or *always,* as it says in the original – this surely is the very fullness of all our joy!

Has not the Lord, however, been always with us? Has He not said, *Lo, I am with you always, even to the end of the age* (Matthew 28:20)? Yes, and the church should not undervalue this nearness, this fellowship. It is no shadow or imagination; it is reality. It is that same reality to which the Lord referred when He said, *He who loves Me will be loved by My Father, and I will love him and will disclose Myself to him* (John 14:21); or as the old versions have it, *will show Mine own self to him.* For when Judas asked the question, *Lord, what then has happened that You are going to disclose Yourself to us and not to the world?* (John 14:22) – that is, "How will it be that the world will not see You, yet we who are living in the world will see You? How is it that we will have Your presence, yet the world will not have it?" – *Jesus answered and said to him, "If anyone loves Me, he will keep My word; and My Father will love him, and We will come to him and make Our abode with him"* (John 14:23). Therefore, we

We have had the Lord always with us.

have had the Lord always with us, even making His abode with us.

It was when we first gave credit to the divine testimony concerning the free love of God, in the gift of His Son, that we drew near to Him and He to us. It was then that He came in unto us and began to dwell with us. It was when we heard His voice and opened the door that He came in to dine with us. It is this conscious presence – this presence that faith realizes – that comforts us amid tribulation here. In the furnace, we have one like the Son of Man to keep us company and to prevent the flame from kindling upon us (Daniel 7:13).

But after all this, it is still incomplete. It is the enjoyment of as much fellowship as can be tasted in absence, but it is no more than that – nor is it intended to take the place of something nearer and more complete, and much less to make us content with absence. No – its tendency is to make us less and less satisfied with absence. It gives us such a desire for a closer relationship that we long for communion that is more unhindered. We want to see Him eye to eye and face to face. This closer communion, this actual vision, this bodily nearness, we are yet to enjoy. The hope given to us is to be with the Lord – with Him in such a way as we have never been before.

Let no one despise this nearness, nor speak evil of it, as if it were material and carnal. Many speak as if their bodies were a curse, as if matter were some piece of miscreation to which we had unnaturally and unhappily been attached. Others tell us that actual interaction such as we refer to, the interaction of vision and voice, is a poor thing not to be named beside the other, which is, as they conceive, deeper and truer.

But is it so? Is matter so despicable? Are our bodies such hindrances to true fellowship? Is the eye nothing, the ear nothing, the smile nothing, the voice nothing, the embrace nothing, and the clasping of the hand nothing? Is personal communion a hindrance to earthly friendships? Can a friend enjoy the communion of friend as well when he is far away as when he is near? Does it not matter to the wife if her husband is unseen and far away? Acknowledging that we can still love and receive love in return, is distance no barrier? Does absence make no void? Do we disregard bodily presence and visible interaction as worthless and almost undesirable? Is not the reverse one of the most deep-seated feelings of our nature, and is it not to this deep-seated feeling that the incarnation appeals? Is that incarnation useless except as furnishing a victim for the altar and providing blood for the cleansing of the worshipper? No. The incarnation brings God near to us in such a way that could not have been done by any other means. He became bone of our bone and flesh of our flesh so that we might have a being like ourselves to commune with, to love, and to lean upon.

In that day when we will be with the Lord, we will know to the full the plan of God in the incarnation of His Son, and we will taste the blessedness of seeing Him as He is. The time of this meeting is His coming, and not until then.

Before that there is distance and imperfection. I know that in the bodiless state there will be greater nearness and fuller enjoyment than now. The apostle Paul longed for this when he had *the desire to depart and be with Christ, for that is very much better* (Philippians 1:23). Even before the resurrection, there is a "being with Christ" that is more satisfying than what we enjoy here. It is a "being with Christ" that is truly *very much better*. I would not want to minimize this blessedness, but still this is not to be compared with resurrection nearness and resurrection fellowship, for then, in a way that up until that time is unknown, we will be introduced into the very presence of the King. All distance will be annihilated, all fellowship will be completed, all joy will be realized, all coldness will be done away, all shadows will be dissipated, and *so we shall always be with the Lord* (1 Thessalonians 4:17).

However, to better understand this subject, let us look at the way in which the apostle handles it in administering comfort to the Thessalonian church, some of whom had been giving way to immoderate grief for the dead.

The grief of the heathen was immoderate, and their expressions of it were equally so. It is no wonder, though. Their hearts beat with as firm a pulse as ours, and natural affection was as strong with them as with us. The husband mourned the wife, and the wife mourned the husband. The parent mourned the child, and the child mourned the parent. Friends wept over the grave of friends. The breaking of these ties was bitter, and the special sting was that they had no hope of reunion. Death to them was a parting forever. It was not as when one parts in the morning to meet again in the evening, or even as when one parts this year to meet a few years later. It was a hopeless separation. At best, it was a vague uncertainty to which deep grief gives no heed. More commonly, it was despair. Their sorrow was desperate and their wound was incurable.

The Thessalonian saints were sorrowing as those who had no hope (1 Thessalonians 4:13), as if they had buried their beloved brethren in an eternal tomb. The apostle Paul reproves them for this. He points out the hope – a sure hope, a blessed hope, a hope able to bring true comfort. *God will bring with Him those who have fallen asleep in Jesus* (1 Thessalonians 4:14). They are not lost. They have only been laid to sleep by Jesus, and He will awaken them when He returns and will bring them up out of their tombs. Their departure cannot be called dying, for it is only sleeping. It has nothing of the despair of death about it. Death has lost its sting. The burial clothes have lost their gloom. The grave has lost its terrors. It is an end of pain. It is a ceasing from toil. *Blessed are the dead who die in the Lord*, for they *rest from their labors* (Revelation 14:13).

The apostle looks beyond the resting place. *Your brother will rise again* (John 11:23). God Himself will unearth their grave and call them up at the return of Him who is *the resurrection and the life* (John 11:25). And this, he says, *We say to you by the word of the Lord* (1 Thessalonians 4:15). He gives this consolation to them as a certainty. There is nothing in it that is vague or doubtful. It is a certainty proclaimed by himself and resting on the Lord's own words to His disciples before He left the earth regarding His return and the gathering of His elect to Him. The Lord is to come! This is the certainty. The Lord will come, and in that coming are wrapped up all the hopes of His saints.

There will be two classes of these saints when He comes: (1) Those who *are alive and remain*; the last generation of the church. For, says the apostle elsewhere, *We will not all sleep, but we will all be changed* (1 Corinthians 15:51). (2) *Those who have fallen asleep;* these form the larger number, no doubt, for the

The Lord is to come!

sleeping ones of all ages will be there. It might be supposed that the living ones would have the advantage since they are alive when the Lord arrives, but no, it is not so. They may have some advantages, though. They never taste death. They are like Enoch and Elijah. They do not know the grave. They see no corruption. In their case, soul and body are never separated. They do not meet the king of terrors, nor fall under his power.

In volume 17 of his *Works*, Richard Baxter wrote:

> Would it not rejoice your hearts if you were sure to live to see the coming of the Lord, and to see His glorious appearing and procession? If you were not to die, but were to be caught up to meet the Lord, would you be opposed to this? Would it not be the greatest joy that you could desire? For my own part, I must confess to you that death, as death, appears to me as an enemy, and my nature does abhor and fear it. However, the thoughts of the coming of the Lord are most sweet and joyful to me, so that

if I were only sure that I would live to see it, and that the trumpet would sound, the dead would rise, and the Lord would appear before the period of my age, it would be the most joyful news to me in the world. Oh, that I might see His kingdom come! It is the character of His saints to love His appearing and to look for that blessed hope. *The Spirit and the bride say, Come* (Revelation 22:17). *Amen. Come, Lord Jesus* (Revelation 22:20). "Come quickly" is the voice of faith and hope and love, but I do not find that His servants are characterized by their desire to die. It is therefore the presence of their Lord that they desire, but it is death that they abhor. Therefore, although they can submit to death, it is the coming of Christ that they love and long for. If death is the last enemy to be destroyed at the resurrection, we may learn how earnestly believers should long and pray for the second coming of Christ, when this full and final conquest will be made. There is something in death that is corrective, even to believers – but in the coming of Christ and their resurrection, there is nothing but glorifying grace.

These are privileges, yet on the other hand, it might be said that these saints do not taste the gladness of resurrection, that they are not conformed to their Lord in this because He died and rose. Still, the end in both cases is the same. The one will have no advantage and no preeminence over the other. Both are able to *stand in the presence of His glory blameless with great joy* (Jude 1:24). Both are equally blameless, although each has undergone a different process for accomplishing this. Thus, the one being changed and the other raised, they are formed into one company, marshaled into one mighty army, and then caught up into the clouds to meet the Lord in the air.

Let us briefly look into the details of this coming, insofar as the apostle gives them. *The Lord Himself will descend from heaven* (1 Thessalonians 4:16). The same Jesus who ascended, He who loved us and washed us from our sins in His own blood, He – His own self – will come, and will come in the same way as He was seen going into heaven. *With a shout.* This is the shout of a monarch's procession, the shout of a great army. Just as Jesus is said to have gone up with shouts, so He is to return with the shout of the conqueror, the shout of triumph. *The voice of the archangel.* A solitary voice is then heard making some mighty announcement, such as that of the angel standing upon sea and earth, proclaiming that *there will be delay no longer* (Revelation 10:6); or of that other angel, with whose glory the earth was illumined, crying with a loud voice, *Fallen, fallen is Babylon the great!* (Revelation 18:2); or of that other angel, who cried with a loud voice to all the fowls of heaven, *Come, assemble for the great supper of God* (Revelation 19:17). *The trumpet of God.* It is elsewhere called *the last trumpet* (1 Corinthians 15:52). It is God's own trumpet, the trumpet that awakes the dead. It is not merely a voice – as if that were too feeble for such a purpose, nor a common trumpet, but the trumpet of God, one that can pierce the grave and awaken the dead.

These are the steps and the accompaniments of the Lord's coming. There is first the shout of the angelic host as the Redeemer leaves His seat above to take possession of His kingdom here. This shout is continued as He descends. Then, as He approaches nearer, the multitude of the heavenly host is silent, and a solitary voice is heard – the voice of the archangel declaring God's message. Then comes the trumpet that calls forth the sleeping just. They obey the call. They arise. No holy dust remains behind. They put on immortality. Then, joined by the transfigured and glorified living, they hasten upward to the embrace of their beloved Lord.

It is into the clouds that they are caught up (1 Thessalonians 4:17). That cloud, or clouds, which in all likelihood rested above Eden, making it the place of *the presence of the* LORD (Genesis 3:8), appeared to Moses at the bush, led Israel over the Red Sea and through the desert, covered Sinai, dwelt in the tabernacle and in the temple, was seen by Isaiah, was described by Ezekiel, shined down upon the Son of God at His baptism and transfiguration, received Him out of sight at His ascension, was seen by Stephen when he was breathing out his soul, smote Saul to the ground on his way to Damascus, and last of all, appeared to John in Patmos. We know that this cloud will reappear in the latter day. It is into this cloud of the divine presence, this symbol of the excellent glory, Jehovah's tent or dwelling place, the ark of our safety against the flood of fire, that the saints will be caught up when the Lord appears, and the voice is heard from heaven, *You who lie in the dust, awake and shout for joy* (Isaiah 26:19). As it was said in Israel, *The song to the LORD also began with the trumpets* (2 Chronicles 29:27), even so will our resurrection song begin with the trumpet of God.

It is with songs that we will go up on high. Our *songs in the night* (Job 35:10) will be exchanged for the songs of the morning. They will be *songs of deliverance* with which we will then be surrounded by in that day when we get up into our *hiding place* to be preserved from trouble (Psalm 32:7). They will be songs of deliverance when we enter into our rooms and close our doors behind us until the *indignation runs its course* (Isaiah 26:20). We will

It is with songs that we will go up on high.

no longer sing our songs in a strange land or by the rivers of Babylon (Psalm 137:1). We will no longer make melody in the house of our pilgrimage (Psalm 119:54) or in the wilderness, but in the King's own presence, in the great congregation, in the new Jerusalem, which comes down out of heaven from God (Revelation 21:2). Then, standing upon the sea of glass and beholding the judgments of God that have been revealed, as Israel did when Pharaoh and his chariots sank like lead in the mighty waters, we sing the song of Moses and the song of the Lamb (Revelation 15:2-4).

Therefore, *caught up* into the cloud, we *meet the Lord in the air* (1 Thessalonians 4:17), as those do who go forth to meet a friend who is already on his way to them. We meet Him in order that, being there acquitted, acknowledged, and confessed by Him before His Father and before the angels, we may form His procession and come with Him to execute vengeance, to judge the world, to share His triumphs, and to reign with Him in His glorious kingdom (Zechariah 14:5; 1 Thessalonians 3:13; Jude 1:14; Revelation 3:21).

After meeting the Lord in this way, we are to be always with Him (1 Thessalonians 4:17). He will be with us, and we will be with Him forever. *So we shall always be with the Lord*. As we then shall meet, so we shall never part. As is our meeting, so is our eternal communion, our continuance in the presence of His glory. We will see Him face to face (1 Corinthians 13:12), and His name will be on our foreheads (Revelation 22:4). Sitting upon the same throne, dwelling under the same roof, hearing His voice, having free access to Him at all times, doing His will, going forth on His errands – this will be the joy of our eternity.

There will be no distance, for that is eradicated. There will be no separation, for that is among the things that are absolutely impossible. There will be no cloud between us, for that is swept away and cannot reappear. There will be no coldness, for love is always full. There will be no interruption, for who can come between the Bridegroom and the bride? There will be no change, for He makes us like Himself, without variableness. There will be no parting, for we have reached our home to go out no more. There will be no end, for the duration of our fellowship is the life of the Ancient of Days, of Him who is *from everlasting to everlasting* (Psalm 90:2).

With the Lord (1 Thessalonians 4:17)! It would be

much to be with Enoch, Abraham, Moses, Elijah, or Paul. It would be much to share their fellowship, to talk with them about the things of God and the story of their own wondrous lives. How much more, though, to be *with the Lord*! How wondrous it would have been to be like Peter at His side, like Mary at His feet, or like John leaning on Him; to have met Him in the streets of Jerusalem, by the sea of Galilee, or at Jacob's well; to have heard Him name your name and greet you as He passed by with the wish of "peace;" to have dwelt in the next house to His at Nazareth, to have been the guest at the table of Lazarus when He was there, to have slept under that roof, perhaps in the room next to the Lord of glory! How much we would have valued privileges such as these, treasuring them in our memory like gold! Yes, how wondrous it is even to hear the tidings of His love, to have a message from Him, to be told that He was gracious to us and kept us in mind, to be anywhere beyond the reach of sin and pain! Oh, how incredibly wondrous it must be to be with the Lord – with Him in His glory; with Him as a friend is with a friend; with Him as the bride is with the bridegroom, saying without fear or hesitation, *May he kiss me with the kisses of his mouth! For your love is better than wine* (Song of Solomon 1:2), and hearing Him say in return:

> *You are altogether beautiful, my darling,*
> *and there is no blemish in you. Come with*
> *me from Lebanon, my bride, may you come*
> *with me from Lebanon. Journey down from*
> *the summit of Amana, from the summit*

> *of Senir and Hermon, from the dens of*
> *lions, from the mountains of leopards. You*
> *have made my heart beat faster, my sister,*
> *my bride; you have made my heart beat*
> *faster with a single glance of your eyes,*
> *with a single strand of your necklace. How*
> *beautiful is your love, my sister, my bride!*
> *How much better is your love than wine!*
> (Song of Solomon 4:7-10)

Always with the Lord (1 Thessalonians 4:17)! This soothes all sorrow and sums up all joy. If even here we can say so gladly and so surely, *I am convinced that neither death, nor life, nor angels, nor principalities, nor things present, nor things to come, nor powers, nor height, nor depth, nor any other created thing, will be able to separate us from the love of God, which is in Christ Jesus our Lord* (Romans 8:38-39), how much more gladly and surely we will be able to say it then!

> Forever to behold Him shine,
> Forevermore to call Him mine![8]

This is what we look for. This is our watchword and our song, even in the day of absence and sorrow. It is this that makes the expected morning so truly a morning of joy. *As for me, I shall behold Your face in righteous-ness; I will be satisfied with Your likeness when I awake* (Psalm 17:15).

---

8 This is from a hymn by Joseph Swain (1761-1796) that begins with "Oh, how the thought that I shall know."

Chapter 10

The Kingdom

That to which the *many tribulations* lead us is a kingdom (Acts 14:22). It is to this that it ministers an abundant entrance (2 Peter 1:11) – an entrance that in itself is indeed not joyous, but grievous, yet is glorious once the entrance has been gone through.

Up until now it has been midnight and the wilderness; before long it will be morning and the kingdom. For it is *in the morning* that the righteous *shall rule* (Psalm 49:14). Just as the night has been the time of being downtrodden and wearing out, so the morning is the time of having dominion and of bringing judgment to light (Zephaniah 3:5). When the Just One will rule over men, he will be *as the light of the morning when the sun rises, a morning without clouds* (2 Samuel 23:3-4). The time when *God will help* is *when morning dawns* (Psalm 46:5). At evening there is trouble, but *before morning they are no more* (Isaiah 17:14). The reign of Antichrist is over, and the reign of Christ begins. The kingdom of the unrighteous is broken to pieces, and the kingdom of the righteous rises in its place. Lucifer, the pretended light-bringer, the false son of the morning, vanishes from the heavens, and the true Light, *the bright morning star* (Revelation 22:16), takes His place in the firmament, unclouded and unsetting in His glory. *Then the sovereignty, the dominion and the greatness of all the kingdoms under the whole heaven will be given to the people of the saints of the Highest One* (Daniel 7:27). The church's weary burden is no longer *How long, O LORD?* (Psalm 13:1), but *The LORD reigns, let the earth rejoice* (Psalm 97:1). Her prayer, *Your kingdom come* (Matthew 6:10; Luke 11:2), is exchanged for the thanksgiving of the *loud voices in heaven*, saying, *The kingdom of the world has become the kingdom of our Lord and of His Christ* (Revelation 15:11). *We give You thanks, O Lord God, the Almighty, who are and who were [and who is to come], because You have taken Your great power and have begun to reign* (Revelation 11:17). *Hallelujah! For the Lord our God, the Almighty, reigns* (Revelation 19:6).

That to which we are hastening on is a royal inheritance – a kingdom.

That to which we are hastening on is not merely an inheritance, but it is a *royal* inheritance – a kingdom. That for which we suffer is a crown. If we suffer, *we will also reign with Him* (2 Timothy 2:12). As we have been truly fellow sufferers, so we will be as truly fellow reigners. The suffering has been real, and so will the reigning be. This is the recompense of reward (Hebrews 10:35) to which we have respect when we choose rather to suffer affliction *with the people of God than to enjoy the passing pleasures of sin* (Hebrews 11:25). This is the *better possession and a lasting one* for which we are willing to endure the *great conflict of sufferings* (Hebrews 10:32, 34). This is the summing up of earth's toil and grief, the issue of a lifetime's conflict with weariness, wrong, and sin.

To think of trial as a preparation for the kingdom is good, but to look at it as an entrance into the kingdom is even better. At the end of time's dark avenue stands the mansion house, the palace! At the edge of our desert path lies the kingdom! The avenue may be rugged under foot, thorny on every side, and gloomy overhead, and the wilderness may be *a howling waste* (Deuteronomy 32:10), yet they are passages – entrances. They are not endless, and their end is gladness. They usher us into a state that will, in a moment, erase the bitter past so that it *will not be remembered or come to mind* (Isaiah 65:16). Thus, although in one aspect tribulation seems to be a path or gateway fenced with brier bushes and hard to fight through, yet in another sense it is the conqueror's triumphal arch under which we pass into the kingdom – so that while passing through, we can sing the song of Him who long ago went this way before us: *I consider that the sufferings of this present time are not worthy to be compared with the glory that is to be revealed to us* (Romans 8:18).

The thought of the kingdom uplifts us, and the stray gleams of it that faith gives us are like the lattice lights of a loved dwelling, sparkling through the thicket to the weary eye of a wanderer who has been overtaken by the dark. Yes, we are heirs of nothing less than a kingdom, no matter how unlike that we may seem at present, and no matter how unrealistic it may be considered to claim so much and to aspire so high. Robes of royalty will soon cover all our coarseness, and beneath the glory of a throne we will bury all our poverty, shame, and grief.

However, this is not all. The various virtues of that kingdom, as made known to us by prophets and apostles, are such as especially meet our case and contrast with our present condition. This appropriateness, this contrast, makes the thoughts of the kingdom doubly precious and comforting.

It is the kingdom of God (1 Corinthians 6:9). Man's kingdoms have passed away. Those kingdoms under which the saints of God have been trodden down have passed away. All that is man's is gone, and nothing remains except what is God's! The glory of the kingdom is that it is entirely God's. It must, then, be perfect and blessed, completely unlike anything that these eyes of ours have seen. If it were only a reformation of human kingdoms, if it were a mere change of government, the expectation of it would be only doubtful comfort. However, it is an entire passing away of the old and making all things new. It is the return of God to His own world, and oh, what will not that return do for us! His re-enthronement is what we desire, for it is this alone that gives us the assurance of perpetuity and stability against which no enemy will prevail. It was to that re-enthronement that Jesus looked forward when He was about to ascend the cross, and of which He spoke about twice at the Passover table (Luke 22:16, 18), as if this were *the joy set before Him*, because of which He *endured the cross, despising the shame* (Hebrews 12:2). It is that re-enthronement that we also anticipate as the day of our triumph, for then we will *shine forth as the sun in the kingdom of [our] Father* (Matthew 13:43).

It is the kingdom of Christ (Colossians 1:13). This assures that we will feel at home there. It is not a stranger who is to seat us on the throne beside Him, but our nearest of kin, the Man who died for us. It is the pierced hands that hold the scepter. This answers our case. We are strangers here, particularly feeling not at home in the courts and palaces of earth, but then it will be otherwise. Here we are as people standing outside the kingdoms of the world. They belong to the prince of this world (John 14:30), but not to Christ, and therefore not to us. They do not greet us with any friendly welcome. They have no honors for us. They make us stand outside. They are to us what Pilate, Herod, and Annas were to Jesus. They call for us to be wronged and smitten, or at least they look on while we endure tribulation, distress, persecution, famine, nakedness, peril, and sword (Romans 8:35).

Much of the church's tribulation has arisen from the kingdoms of this world not being Christ's. But in the age to come, Christ is to reign, all things being put in subjection to Him. He who is to reign knows what it is to be hated by the world, and therefore, He knows how to make up to us, in His kingdom, for all the hatred with which we have been hated, and for all the sorrow that has weighed us down while here. This is obviously the point of Christ's declaration to His disciples, for having said to them, *You are those who have stood by Me in My trials,* He adds, *and just as My Father has granted Me a kingdom, I grant you that you may eat and drink at My table in My kingdom, and you will sit on thrones judging the twelve tribes of Israel* (Luke 22:28-30), thus linking together present suffering *for* Christ and future reigning *with* Christ – present continuance with Him in trial and future association with Him in His own kingdom when He returns to receive the crown.

It is a kingdom not of this world (John 18:36). The words *not of this world* are literally, "not out of, or not taken out of, this world," just as when Christ says, *You are of this world, I am not of this world* (John 8:23). This world is entirely evil and is under the dominion of the Evil One. Its territory is under a curse. It is called this present evil world (Galatians 1:4). It lies in wickedness (1 John 5:19). Its kingdoms are compared to hideous beasts of prey (Daniel 7) – Satan and his hosts, the rulers of the darkness of this world (Ephesians 6:12). Therefore, everything pertaining to it is unholy. The kingdom to come is not made out of its materials so as to retain anything of its likeness. Between the kingdoms of this world and the kingdom of the world to come, there is no harmony or resemblance. It is said about this world that it rejects the Spirit and cannot receive Him (John 14:17), but that world to come is to be full of the Spirit, for the Spirit is to be *poured out upon us from on high, and the wilderness becomes a fertile field* (Isaiah 32:15). Satan is king of this world, but Christ is king of that world. This world does not know God, neither the Father nor the Son; but in that world, all will know Him, from the least to the greatest (Jeremiah 31:34; Hebrews 8:11). In this world, all is darkness; but in that world, all is light. This world is to be fought against and overcome; that world is to be loved and enjoyed. We see, then, that the kingdom of which we are the heirs is as unlike this world as Eden was unlike the wilderness – and it is this that makes it so desirable. If it had retained any fragments of this world's evil, if it had been a

In this world, all is darkness; but in that world, all is light.

mere reconstruction of its worldly elements, if it had taken up into itself any of its corrupt qualities, then our comfort would be poor in anticipating its arrival and counting on the exchange. But it is not of this world, and this is our joy. We have had enough of this world to make us long for its passing away and to welcome a kingdom in which no stain or trace of it will be found.

It is a righteous kingdom. *The kingdom of God is not eating and drinking* – that is, it is not a carnal kingdom made up of outward observances and worldly delights – but it is *righteousness and peace and joy in the Holy Spirit* (Romans 14:17). That is, it is a righteous, peaceful, joyful kingdom, dwelt in and filled by the Holy Spirit so that all belonging to it must be like itself. It is a kingdom whose territory is the *new earth, in which righteousness dwells* (2 Peter 3:13). The unrighteous will not inherit it (1 Corinthians 6:9); but the saints alone will possess it (Daniel 7:18). *A scepter of uprightness is the scepter of Your kingdom* (Psalm 45:6). He who holds the scepter is the righteous King (Isaiah 32:1), and in His days, the righteous will flourish (Psalm 72:7). It is a *crown of righteousness* that is laid up for us (2 Timothy 4:8). Then *the work of righteousness will be peace, and the service of righteousness, quietness and confidence forever* (Isaiah 32:17). The righteousness of this kingdom makes it unspeakably attractive to those who have been worn out with the unrighteousness of an unrighteous world. The thought that the morning is to bring in that righteous kingdom comforts us amid the clouds and thick darkness of this night of weeping.

It is a kingdom of peace. War has by that time run its course. Its spears are broken and turned to plowshares. Strife and hatred have fled. The storm has become a calm, and the troubled sea is still. Holy tranquility breathes over earth. *Let the mountains bring peace to the people, and the hills, in righteousness. . . . In his days may the righteous flourish, and abundance of peace till the moon is no more* (Psalm 72:3, 7). *To David and his descendants and his house and his throne, may there be peace from the LORD forever* (1 Kings 2:33). Far more truly than in the days of Solomon there will be *peace on all sides around about* (1 Kings 4:24). Yes, the Lord God will give rest on every side so that there will be *neither adversary nor misfortune* (1 Kings 5:4). The motto that was inscribed upon Gideon's altar, Jehovah Shalom, or *the LORD is Peace* (Judges 6:24), will be inscribed everywhere. The beasts of the field will be at peace with us (Job 5:23), for *the wolf will dwell with the lamb, and the leopard will lie down with the young goat, and the calf and the young lion and the fatling together; and a little boy will lead them. Also the* *cow and the bear will graze, their young will lie down together. . . . They will not hurt or destroy in all My holy mountain* (Isaiah 11:6-7, 9). The groans of creation will then be over, and its deliverance accomplished. All will be peace, for the great Peacemaker is come. He is the *king of Salem*, or the *king of peace* (Hebrews 7:2). He is called the *Prince of Peace* (Isaiah 9:6), and *there will be no end to the increase of His government or of peace* (Isaiah 9:6-7).

With what longing hearts we desire the arrival of that kingdom that is so unlike what this troubled earth has yet known from the beginning until now. Each new sorrow stirs the longing. Each new conflict makes us glad at the thought that there is such a kingdom in reserve. If it were not for this, how we would *fret because of evildoers* (Psalm 37:1), and how soon would our patience give way! However, with our eye upon this kingdom of peace, we can glory in tribulation (Romans 5:3), we can drink the bitterest cup, we can face the thickest storm, and we can endure the harshest tumult – and when the world's uproar grows loudest, we can lift up our heads, knowing that our *redemption is drawing near* (Luke 21:28).

It is a kingdom that cannot be moved (Hebrews 12:28). All other kingdoms have not only been moved, but they have been shaken to pieces. Great *Babylon, the beauty of kingdoms* (Isaiah 13:19), has been a sand wreath, raised by one tide and leveled by the next. So have all others been, greater or lesser. One by one they have been overthrown and crushed, or they have crumbled down and become like the chaff of the summer threshing floor. However, the kingdom that we look for is *the eternal kingdom of our Lord and Savior Jesus Christ* (2 Peter 1:11). It abides forever. Neither force nor age can affect it. It rises out of the ruins of earth's present empires, although it is unlike them all. The things that can decay or become moldy are shaken in order that they may be shaken off, and so those things that cannot be shaken may remain. Thus there comes forth the immovable kingdom, the kingdom into which sin does not enter; in which change has no place; into which the curse does not consume; of which wisdom and holiness are the strong pillars; where corruption is unknown; where order triumphs; and of which the glory never dims.

It is joy to us in such a world of instability and commotion to think of such a kingdom. Driven to and fro with the changes of the kingdoms we inhabit here, and wearied with the falling and the rising, the casting down and the building up, we long for a kingdom that will give us rest – a kingdom that cannot be moved. How many of our griefs have come from this uncertainty and unreliability! What is there so dreary and so dreadful as the thought that every inch of ground beneath us is shifting, that every prop upon which we lean is breaking, that every twig to which we cling is snapping? As we draw our curtains around us, we do not know what change, what loss, and what sorrow will greet us tomorrow. Or if we go through the morning lighthearted and unburdened, we tremble to think what clouds may have gathered over our dwelling before the evening has fallen.

Such is the perishableness, the changeableness, of earth and its kingdoms! What joy it is to look beyond them all and see the everlasting kingdom through their shadows! What joy it is to be assured that this kingdom is at hand, and that before long He *with whom there is no variation or shifting shadow* (James 1:17) will welcome us to its unchanging rest, and that He who is *the same yesterday and today and forever* (Hebrews 13:8) will seat us upon the eternal throne.

Samuel Rutherford said, "Heaven is but a company of noble venturers for Christ," and we may add, "of noble sufferers too." Of such is the kingdom of heaven! It is in that kingdom that we will rest from our labors and find the end of all our sufferings. We will find that we have not risked too much, labored too much, or suffered too much. The glory of the kingdom will make up for it all.

Do not be afraid, little flock, for your Father has chosen gladly to give you the kingdom (Luke 12:32). Along with the *King of glory* (Psalm 24:8-10), we will take our place upon the throne, in that day when, after raising the

The glory of the kingdom will make up for it all.

poor from the dust, He will set them among princes and have them inherit the throne of glory; when the wicked will be silenced in darkness and the adversaries of the Lord will be broken in pieces; when *the LORD will judge the ends of the earth*, giving strength to His king, and exalting *the horn of His anointed* (1 Samuel 2:8-10).

Your kingdom come (Matthew 6:10; Luke 11:2). This is the burden of our cries. Weary of man's rule, we long for God's. Sick at heart with this world's scenes of evil – man harming man; man enslaving man; man wounding man; man defrauding man; man treading upon man – we long for the setting up of the righteous throne. Oh, what a world this will be when man's will as well as man's rule will be exchanged for Christ's rule and will; when God's will shall be done on earth even as it is done in heaven (Matthew 6:10)!

It is our joy to think that this kingdom is near and that there are no centuries of sin and wrong still in reserve either for the church or for the earth. Its nearness is our comfort. The hope that it will come encourages us, but the thought that it is coming soon uplifts us more, for both faith and hope are fed by the thought of nearness. We do not agonize at delay, nor do we grow weak and downhearted; yet in some respects, our feelings are not unlike those thus described by one of other days:

> So tedious is this day,
> As is the night before some festival
> To an impatient child that hath new robes,
> And may not wear them.[9]

Our bridal robes are ready, and we long to put them on. Our priestly royal raiment is also ready, and we desire to exchange for it these weeds of poverty, shame, and widowhood. Yet in patience we possess our souls (Luke 21:19).

We are on the daily lookout for a kingdom, lifting

---

9   This is from Act III, Scene II of William Shakespeare's *Romeo and Juliet*.

up our heads knowing that our *redemption is drawing near* (Luke 21:28). *It will not delay* (Habakkuk 2:3). The signs of its approach are multiplying. The shadows are still passing and repassing along the gray cliffs, but their increasing rapidity of movement shows a momentous change at hand. Kingdoms are still rising as well as falling, but the deep force of the forewarnings – the brevity as well as the abruptness of change – indicates a crisis. At this crisis, the world's movements are brought to a standstill. Then, touched by a divine hand, they start up again. A better order of rule begins. Satan has been bound (Revelation 20:1-3). *The oppressor has ceased* (Isaiah 14:4). He who smote the people in wrath is smitten (Isaiah 14:5-6). The misgoverned world rejoices. *The whole earth is at rest and is quiet; they break forth into shouts of joy* (Isaiah 14:7). The anointed King has appeared. The great kingdom has come!

Chapter 11

The Grace

Our fountainhead of blessing here is grace. It was to this grace, the free love of God, that we came when the consciousness of want and sin first awoke within us. We found this grace of God to be large enough for us and entirely suitable, so that while we felt ourselves unfit objects for anything else, because of that, we were just the more fit objects for grace. We were fit for either wrath or for grace, but for nothing else – for nothing between. We retreated from the wrath, and we took refuge in the grace. Between the one and the other, the blood of the accepted sacrifice has made a way, a way of holiness (Isaiah 35:8). We saw that way. We saw it to be free and unchallenged. We fled along that way, and soon found ourselves beyond the reach of wrath and under the broad covering of grace – under the very wing of the gracious One – of Him who is *full of grace and truth* (John 1:14).

It was the knowledge of this grace that removed

our doubts, quieted our fears, and made us blush for our unbelief and suspicious mistrust. It is the knowledge of this grace that still keeps our souls in peace, in spite of weakness, sin, and conflict. Being permitted to draw upon it without limit and without restriction, we feel that no circumstances can arise in which we will not be at liberty to use it, and in which it is not our principal sin to stand distant from it, as if it had become less wide and free. With all this abundant grace placed at our disposal, to draw upon continually, what foolishness it is to be afraid of enemies, evils, and days of trouble! For the prophet Jeremiah says, *Blessed is the man who trusts in the* LORD *and whose trust is the* LORD. *For he will be like a tree planted by the water, that extends its roots by a stream and will not fear when the heat comes; but its leaves will be green, and it will not be anxious in a year of drought nor cease to yield fruit* (Jeremiah 17:7-8).

It is in grace that we continue.

It is in this grace that we continue (Acts 13:43). It is in this grace that we stand (Romans 5:2). It is in this grace that we are to be strong (2 Timothy 2:1). It is this grace that we are to hold fast (Hebrews 12:28). It is this grace that is sufficient for us (2 Corinthians 12:9). It is this grace that we desire for others, saying, "The grace of our Lord Jesus Christ be with you" (Ephesians 6:24; 2 Corinthians 13:14). All is grace, from the beginning to the end. It is pure grace, in which no respect is had to anything of good that has been done, felt, thought, or spoken by us. The history of our life is wrapped up in these blessed words: *Where sin increased, grace abounded all the more* (Romans 5:20).

We have found that the new sins of each hour, so far from closing the fountain of grace against us, opened new springs of grace for us – springs of grace that we would never have known otherwise, nor thought it possible to exist. It is not as if sin were less vile because of this. David's horrid sins were the occasions of opening up new depths of grace that were unimagined before, yet his iniquity lost none of its hatefulness because of this. Grace is always gushing forth upon us to sweep away each new sin, yet in doing so, it makes the sin that is swept away appear more hideous and inexcusable. The brighter the sun, the darker and sharper are the shadows; and the fuller the grace, the viler the sin appears.

As our personal history, as saved people, is the history of abundant sin met by more abundant grace, so is the general history of all things in this fallen world. What is all of Israel's history, every step of it, but the history of man's immense sin drawing out the more immense grace of God? What is the church's history but the same, so that each of the chosen and called ones who make up its mighty multitude can say with him of old, whose name was chief of sinners, *The grace of our Lord was more than abundant, with the faith and love which are found in Christ Jesus* (1 Timothy 1:14-15). What is even the history of this material creation, on which the curse has pressed so long and heavily, but the history of grace abounding over sin and rescuing this polluted soil from the devouring fire?

All has been of grace up until now, and all will be of grace in the future, too. In this respect there will be no change, yet this is not the whole truth, for the brightest disclosures are still to come. The first coming of the Lord opened up to us heights and depths of most wondrous grace, but His second coming will bring with it discoveries of grace just as marvelous and as yet unrevealed. That promise, *The LORD gives grace and glory* (Psalm 84:11), seems specifically to refer to the time when, after days of sad longing (Psalm 84:2) and weary journeying through the valley of Baca (Psalm 84:6), we appear in Zion before God. Then, standing in the new Jerusalem, we sing the song of blessed contrast: *A day in Your courts is better than a thousand outside* (Psalm 84:10) – as if this new outburst of grace, which meets us as we enter the gates of pearl, surpasses all that we had tasted before.

The apostle Peter also points forward to the same period for the full display of grace when he speaks of the grace that is to be brought to us *at the revelation of Jesus Christ* (1 Peter 1:13), indicating to us that in that day, new and larger circles of grace will open out, just as the horizon widens when the sun ascends. The prophet Zechariah points to this same day when he says, *He will bring forth the top stone with shouts of "Grace, grace to it!"* (Zechariah 4:7). However, this truth is especially taught to us by the apostle Paul when he tells us that God's purpose in making us alive together with Christ, in raising us up together and making us sit together in heavenly places, is that *in the ages to come He might show the surpassing riches of His grace in kindness toward us in Christ Jesus* (Ephesians 2:5-7). Here he piles up word upon word, as if he could not find any strong enough for his purpose. It is not merely *grace*, but it is *riches of grace*; it is not only this, but it is *surpassing riches of grace* – riches of grace not only surpassing all other riches, but surpassing all those riches of grace that have previously been known, as if past grace were to be forgotten in the abundance of that which is to come.

How often in Israel's past days, when sin abounded, has grace come pouring in, obliterating the sin as if it had never been! But in the day when the Redeemer will come to Zion and turn away ungodliness from Jacob (Isaiah 59:20), at the moment when their cry of despair may be, *Has God forgotten to be gracious?* (Psalm 77:9), grace will come in upon them like a flood, fuller and richer than anything that they or their fathers knew, tearing down mightier obstacles and leveling higher mountains of iniquity. In reference to this time, it is written, *Therefore the Lord longs to be gracious to you, and therefore He waits on high to have compassion on you. . . . He will surely be gracious to you at the sound of your cry* (Isaiah 30:18-19). In that day, grace will not merely bring forgiveness to Israel, but will also raise her to a height of glory in the earth and eminence among the nations so that the past *will not be remembered or come to mind* (Isaiah 65:17).

How often in the church's history has grace been magnified! Each age has brought out to view new wonders of grace, because of which she has praised the God of all grace. However, the abundance of the past is not all that is in store for her. Her returning Lord will bring with Him all the *surpassing riches of His grace*, and these will all be spent on her. When caught up into the clouds to meet her Lord in the air and to be forever with Him (1 Thessalonians 4:17), she will be led into the treasure house of grace and get a glimpse of its vastness. Each step in her past course has drawn forth a fresh outpouring of abundant grace. Grace found her in the *desert land, and in the howling waste of a wilderness* (Deuteronomy 32:10). Grace drew her *out of the pit of destruction, out of the miry clay* (Psalm 40:2). Grace washed her, clothed her, shod her, covered her, and adorned her with ornaments (Ezekiel 16:9-11), giving her beauty for ashes, the oil of joy for mourning, and the garments of praise for the spirit of heaviness (Isaiah 61:3). Grace strengthened her for warfare, hardship, and labor, making her more than conqueror through Him who loved her (Romans 8:37). Grace comforted her in the evil day, wiped away tears, poured in fresh joys, and threw the everlasting arms around her. Grace taught her to pray, praise, love, trust, and serve in spite of the ever-revolting heart within. Grace kept her as a stranger and a pilgrim here, without a city and without a resting place on earth, looking for the city of foundations (Hebrews 11:10), watching for her Lord's appearing amid all the heartsickness of hope deferred (Proverbs 13:12), and wearying for the Bridegroom's embrace, unimpressed and undistracted by the false splendor of a present evil world. But the grace that has brought her this far has not run out, for it is absolutely limitless, like the heart of Him out of whom it comes.

As it raises the church from one level to another, its own circle is ever increasing.

The resurrection dawn, the morning of joy, brings with it new stores of grace. We had thought that grace could go no farther than it had gone here – in forgiving so many sins and in saving us with so complete a salvation – but we then will find that grace had only begun to display itself.

It was only the first sip from the deep well that we tasted here. Grace meets us as we come up from the tomb to supply us with new blessings such as eye has not seen nor ear heard (1 Corinthians 2:9). It clothes us with the royal raiment. It seats us upon the throne. It gives us the *crown of life* (Revelation 2:10), the *crown of righteousness* (2 Timothy 4:8). It makes us pillars in the temple of our God. It writes upon us

> *The resurrection dawn, the morning of joy, brings with it new stores of grace.*

the name of our God and the name of the city of our God (Revelation 3:12). It gives us *the morning star* (Revelation 2:28). It gives us the white stone, and in the stone a new name written that no one knows except he who receives it. It makes us to eat of the *hidden manna* (Revelation 2:17). It leads us back to *the tree of life which is in the Paradise of God* (Revelation 2:7). It brings us into the bridal chamber. It sets us down at the marriage table, teaching us to sing, *Let us rejoice and be glad and give the glory to Him, for the marriage of the Lamb has come and His bride has made herself ready* (Revelation 19:7). It carries us into the midst of that city that has no need of the sun or of the moon to shine in it (Revelation 21:23), whose wall is of jasper, whose foundations are gems, whose gates are pearls, and whose streets are translucent gold (Revelation 21:19-21). It gives us to drink of the pure *river of the water of life, clear as crystal, coming from the throne of God and of the Lamb* (Revelation 22:1).

Grace is still to do all these things for us in that morning that is to dawn when this night of weeping is at an end. All this glory – this exceeding and *eternal weight of glory* (2 Corinthians 4:17) – we will owe to the exceeding riches of that grace that is then so marvelously to unfold itself, heaping honor upon honor, gift upon gift, and joy upon joy without end forever.

Let us notice the difference in this between Christ and His church, the Bridegroom and the bride. The same glory fills both, but the way of receiving it is widely different. To Him it is a reward of righteousness, but to her it is a reward of grace. Righteousness crowns Him, but grace crowns her. These marvelous honors are the claim of righteousness in His case, but the mere award of grace in hers. Of Him it is written, *You have loved righteousness and hated wickedness; therefore God, Your God, has anointed You with the oil of joy above Your fellows* (Psalm 45:7); while of her it is said, *Who has saved us and called us with a holy calling, not according to our works, but according to His own purpose and grace which was granted us in Christ Jesus from all eternity* (2 Timothy 1:9). What righteousness does for Him, grace does for her. And oh, how measureless must that grace be when it can do for her all that righteousness can do for Him!

That coming day of grace sheds light upon the present by showing us how vast and inexhaustible that grace is that is pouring itself out from the heart of the Father through the blood of the Son. If these riches of grace are so exceedingly great, then how is it possible for us to entertain the suspicion that so often troubles us now: "Is there grace enough for the pardon of sins like mine – grace enough to secure welcome and acceptance to a sinner like me?"

What! Is there grace enough to receive multitudes, washing them clean and presenting them blameless in the day of the Lord with exceeding joy – and is there not enough for one? Is there grace enough to pour out such wondrous glory upon the multitudes of the undeserving in time to come, and is there not enough to bring forgiveness to one undeserving soul just now? In telling of the grace that the ages to come are to unroll, we are proclaiming good news to the chief of sinners – good news concerning the infinite vastness of grace, good news concerning Him out of whom this blessed stream is flowing.

Oh, what a rebuke to fear, to doubt, to suspicion, and to unbelief is the truth concerning these exceeding riches of grace yet to be unfolded! Is it possible that we can go on fearing, doubting, suspecting, and misbelieving – with the assured knowledge that grace is so free and abundant, so sufficient to embrace the entire circumstances of our case, and so suitable to each special need, each special burden, and each particular sin? Will we dare to make more of the sin than of the grace, of the need than of the supply, and of the burden than of the relief? Will we not be ashamed to magnify our sin beyond the grace of God, and to reason as if the grace that can confer on us the kingdom and the crown of Christ were not large enough in scope to cover our sins? Oh, the foolishness of unbelief – foolishness without a name and without an equal – to believe in a grace willing to place us on the throne of the universe by the side of the everlasting Son, yet not willing to pardon us! How foolish to believe in a grace large enough to say, *Come, you who are blessed of My Father, inherit the kingdom prepared for you from the foundation of the world* (Matthew 25:34), yet not large enough to say, *Take courage, son; your sins are forgiven* (Matthew 9:2).

It has not appeared as yet what we will be (1 John 3:2). Yet as the womb of grace knows no miscarriages, we know that *He who began a good work in you will perfect it until the day of Christ Jesus* (Philippians 1:6). The grace has not had full room to expand itself and show all the vastness of its scope. Our life is hidden. Our glory is hidden. Our inheritance is hidden. Our city has not yet come down out of heaven from God. In the pit of Dothan, it did not appear what Joseph was to be. His strange dreams did foretell something, yet who could have thought that he was to sit upon Pharaoh's throne? It did not appear what Ruth was to be when she lived in Moab as a stranger to the true God, or even when she left her home and family to cast in her lot with Israel. That blessed scene of love and faith when *Orpah kissed* and *Ruth clung* (Ruth 1:14), giving forth a heart of no common character, did suggest something, but who could have thought that she was to be a mother in Israel from whom the Messiah was to spring?

We do not now appear as we will. We do not look like kings. Although at times, when we get a glimpse of the promised crown, and when a vision of its nearness passes before us, our face flushes, our eye twinkles, and our walk unconsciously assumes unusual dignity, yet in general we look very much unlike that which we will be. Sometimes the *We do not now appear as we will.* star of nobility – the badge of our order – flashes out from the earthly covering and glistens on our chest, yet this is seldom, although it is more seldom now in these last days than previously. For religion, even the best, has sunk down from its primitive loftiness into a mild, second-rate, inferior thing, and the still-clinging garments of the old man cover or quench every rising ray of anticipated glory.

What different beings grace would make us if we would only allow it! Yet instead of allowing it, we put it away from us, content with only as much of it as will save us from the wrath to come. We turn away from its fullness, as if by embracing it we would stand committed to a far holier walk and higher style of living than we are prepared for.

> *For the grace of God has appeared, bringing salvation to all men, instructing us to deny ungodliness and worldly desires and to live sensibly, righteously and godly in the present age, looking for the blessed hope and*

> *the appearing of the glory of our great God*
> *and Savior, Christ Jesus, who gave Himself*
> *for us to redeem us from every lawless deed,*
> *and to purify for Himself a people for His*
> *own possession, zealous for good deeds.*
> (Titus 2:11-14)

The grace that flowed in upon us during our long night has been abundant and continual, but it is not ended with the night. The morning brings with it new supplies of grace. When that grace displays itself, then it will appear what we really are. Our present form will fall from us. We will stand forth as *heirs of God* (Romans 8:17), and He who has given us grace will also give us glory. He who led us through the night will bring us forth to the joy of the morning.

Chapter 12

The Glory

Not only a person's true life, but a person's true history, begins with his conversion. Up until that time, he is essentially a being without a history. He has no great story to tell. He is only part of a world lying in wickedness, having nothing about him worthy of being recorded.

But from the moment that he is born again, and thus taken out of the masses of the world, he receives a personality as well as a dignity that qualify him for having a history – a history that God can acknowledge as such, and that God Himself will record. From that time on, he has a story to tell that is wondrous and divine, such as angels listen to, and over which there is joy in heaven (Luke 15:7).

There are millions of drops in the wide ocean, yet they are one mingled mass of fluid; none of them has a history. There may be a history of the ocean, but not of its individual drops. However, your drop is beginning to part from the mass. It takes hold of a sunbeam and rises into the firmament. There it gleams in the rainbow or brightens in the hues of sunset. It now has a history. From the moment that it came out of the mass and obtained a personality, it had a story to tell – a story of its own, a story of splendor and beauty.

What various forms are lying concealed in those huge blocks of unquarried rock! What shapes of statuary or architecture are there! Yet they have no history. They can have none. They are only parts of a hideous block in which not one line or curve of beauty is visible. But the noise of hammers is heard. Man lifts up his tool. A single block is severed. Again he lifts up his tool, and it begins to assume a form – until, as stroke after stroke falls on it, and touch after touch smooths and shapes it, the perfect image of the human form is seen, and it seems as if the hand of the artist had only been employed in unwrapping the stony folds from that fair form and awakening it from the slumber of its marble tomb. From the moment that the chisel touched that piece of rock, its history began.

Such is the case of a saint. His history begins from the moment the hand of the Spirit is laid on him to begin the process of separation. He then receives a conscious, outstanding personality that equips him for having a history – a history entirely marvelous, a history whose pages are both written and read in heaven, a history that in its divine brightness spreads over eternity. His true dignity now begins. He is ready to take a place in history. Each event in his life becomes worthy of being recorded. *The righteous will be remembered forever* (Psalm 112:6).

On earth, this history is one of suffering and dishonor, even as was that of the Master; but hereafter, in the kingdom, it is one of glory and honor. "All the time," said John Howe, "from the soul's first conversion, God has been at work upon it, laboring, shaping it, polishing it, spreading His own glory on it, inlaying, enameling it with glory; now at last the whole work is revealed, the curtain is drawn aside, and the blessed soul awakes." Then a new epoch in its history begins.

We do not now know what that history is to be. We know that it will be wondrous, but we cannot imagine how wondrous. We know that it will be very unlike our present one, yet still not separated from it, but linked to it, even springing out of it as its root or seed. Our present life is the *Our present life is the underground state of the plant.*

underground state of the plant; our future life is the germinating, blossoming, and fruit bearing. However, the plant is the same, and the future depends for all its excellency and beauty upon the present. Night is not the shutting up of day, but day is the opening out of night. Day is simply the night in blossom, the expanded petals of some dark, unattractive bud, containing within it glories of which no glimpses have yet reached us here. It is flighty sentiment, as well as false philosophy, to say as one in our day has done, "Night is nobler than day; day is but a motley-colored veil, spread transiently over the infinite bosom of night, hiding from us its purely transparent, eternal deeps."[10] Night is at best only the beauty of death, while day is the beauty of life. It is life, not death, that is beautiful. And if life on earth, in all its various forms and scenes, is so very beautiful, what will it not be hereafter, when it displays itself to the full, transfused throughout all being with an intensity now unknown, as if almost becoming visible by means of the new glory that it will then spread over all creation.

The wise will inherit honor (Proverbs 3:35). *Let the godly ones exult in glory* (Psalm 149:5). They are *vessels of mercy, which He prepared beforehand for glory* (Romans 9:23). That to which we are called is *eternal glory* (1 Peter 5:10). That which we obtain is *salvation which is in Christ Jesus and with it eternal glory* (2 Timothy 2:10). It is to glory that God is *bringing many sons* (Hebrews 2:10), so that as He, through whom we are brought to it, is *crowned with glory and honor* (Hebrews 2:9), so will we be (Hebrews 2:9). We are to *rejoice with joy inexpressible and full of glory* (1 Peter 1:8). We are not only witnesses *of the sufferings of Christ*, but we are also partakers *of the glory that is to be revealed* (1 Peter 5:1). The word of exhortation therefore says, *Keep on rejoicing, so that also at the revelation of His glory you may rejoice with exultation* (1 Peter 4:13). The promise is not only that if we suffer, we will also reign with Him, but, if we suffer with Him, we will *also be glorified with Him* (Romans 8:17).

---

10 This comes from Thomas Carlyle's *Characteristics*. The full sentence says, "In the same sense, too, have Poets sung 'Hymns to the Night'; as if Night were nobler than Day; as if Day were but a small motley-colored veil spread transiently over the infinite bosom of Night, and did but deform and hide from us its purely transparent eternal deeps."

This glory, then, is our portion. It is the better thing that God has provided for us, and because of which He is not ashamed to be called our God (Hebrews 11:16). This is the glory that throws all present suffering into the darkness, making it to be eternally forgotten.

Glory is the concentrated essence of all that is holy, excellent, and beautiful, for all life has its more and its less perfect parts. Its glory is that which is most perfect about it, to which, of course, that which is less perfect has, according to its measure, contributed. Light is the glory of the sun. Transparency is the glory of the stream. The flower is the glory of the plant. The soul is the glory of the man. The face is the glory of the body. This glory is strangely diverse: *There is one glory of the sun, and another glory of the moon, and another glory of the stars; for star differs from star in glory* (1 Corinthians 15:41).

What is really glorious is so hidden, so ravaged, so intermixed with imperfection and corruption here, that Scripture always speaks as if the whole glory were still in reserve, with none of it yet revealed – so that when He came to earth who was the brightness of Jehovah's glory (Hebrews 1:3), He was not recognized as the possessor of such glory. It was hidden. It did not shine. Few eyes saw any glory at all in Him. None saw the extent or greatness of it. Even in His case, it did not appear what He was and what He will be *when He comes to be glorified in His saints* (2 Thessalonians 1:10).

Scripture casts scorn upon that which the world calls glory, as a vain show (Psalm 39:6), *lighter than breath* (Psalm 62:9), *less than nothing and meaningless* (Isaiah 40:17) – while its name for glory is weight or solidity, to which the apostle Paul seems to refer when he speaks of the *weight of glory* (2 Corinthians 4:17).

All that is glorious, whether visible or invisible, material or immaterial, natural or spiritual, must have its birthplace in God. *From Him and through Him and to Him are all things. To Him be the glory forever* (Romans 11:36). All glorious things come forth out of Him and have their seeds, or germs, or patterns in Him. We say of that flower, "How beautiful," but the type of its beauty – the beauty of which it is the faint expression – is in God. We say of the star, "How bright," but the brightness that it represents or declares is in God. It is the same of every object above and beneath, and so especially it will be seen in the objects of glory that will surround us in the kingdom of God. Of each thing there, as of the city itself, it will be said, "It has the glory of God" (Revelation 21:11).

Glory, then, is our inheritance. The best, the richest, the brightest, and the most beautiful of all that is in God of good and rich and bright and beautiful will be ours. The glory that fills heaven above and the glory that spreads over the earth beneath will be ours. But while the glory of the earthly will be ours, yet in a truer sense, the glory of the heavenly will be ours (1 Corinthians 15:40). Already by faith we have taken our place amid heavenly things, being made alive together with Christ, being raised up with Him, and being made to sit with Him in heavenly places (Ephesians 2:5-6).

Thus we have already claimed the heavenly as our own, and having risen with Christ, we set our affection on things above, *not on the things that are on earth*

(Colossians 3:2). Far-ranging dominion will be ours. We will be encompassed, circle beyond circle stretching over the universe with all varying shades and kinds of glory, but it is the heavenly glory that is so truly ours, as the redeemed and the risen. In the midst of that heavenly glory will be the family mansion, the church's dwelling place and palace – our true home for eternity.

Everything that awaits us is glorious. There is an inheritance waiting for us, and it is *an inheritance which is imperishable and undefiled and will not fade away* (1 Peter 1:4). There is a rest, a sabbath-keeping in store for us (Hebrews 4:9), and this rest *will be glorious* (Isaiah 11:10). The kingdom that we claim is a glorious kingdom. The crown that we are to wear is a glorious crown. The city of our habitation is a glorious city.

Everything that awaits us is glorious.

The garments that will clothe us are garments *for glory and for beauty* (Exodus 28:2). Our bodies will be glorious bodies, transformed *into conformity with the body of His glory* (Philippians 3:21). Our society will be that of the glorified. Our songs will be songs of glory. It is said of the region that we are to inhabit that *the glory of God has illumined it, and its lamp is the Lamb* (Revelation 21:23).

The hope of this glory uplifts us. From under a canopy of night, we look out upon these promised scenes of blessedness, and we are comforted. Our dark thoughts are softened down, even when they are not entirely brightened, for day is near, and joy is near, and the warfare is ending. The tear will be dried up, the shame will be lost in the glory, and we will *stand in the presence of His glory blameless with great joy* (Jude 1:24).

Then the fruit of patience and of faith will appear, and the hope we have so long been clinging to will not put us to shame. Then we will triumph and praise. Then we will be avenged on death, pain, and sickness. Then will every wound be more than healed. Egypt no longer enslaves us. Babylon no longer leads us captive. The Red Sea is crossed, the wilderness is passed, Jordan lies behind us, and we are in Jerusalem! There is no more curse. There is no more night. The tabernacle of God is with us. He dwells in that tabernacle, and we dwell with Him.

It is *the God of all grace* who has called us to His eternal glory in Christ Jesus (1 Peter 5:10). It is when the chief Shepherd appears that we *will receive the unfading crown of glory* (1 Peter 5:4). This will be after we *have suffered for a little while*, and by suffering have been made perfect, established, strengthened, and settled (1 Peter 5:10). Suffering is not lost upon us. It prepares us for the glory. The hope of that glory, as well as the knowledge of the discipline through which we are passing, and of the process of preparation going on in us, sustains us and teaches us to exult in our tribulations (Romans 5:3). This is comfort. It is happiness. This might seem strange in the world's eye, but it is not strange in ours! All that the world has is only a poor imitation of happiness and consolation. Ours is real, even now, and how much more hereafter! Nor will a brief delay and a severe conflict lessen the weight of coming glory. Rather, they will add to it – and it is worth waiting for, it is worth suffering for, and it is worth fighting for. It is so sure of coming, and so blessed when it comes.

John Howe said, "The mass of glory is yet in reserve; we are not yet so high as the highest heavens." All this is hanging over us, inviting us on, stirring us up, and loosening us from things present so that the pain of loss, sickness, or bereavement falls more gently on us and tends only to make us less vain and light, and more thoroughly in earnest.

That they may see My glory, the Lord pleaded for His own (John 17:24). This is the essence of it all. As we have seen, there will be other glories, but this is the heart of it all. It is the very utmost that even the Lord of glory could ask for them. Having sought this, He could seek no more. He could go no further. Our response to this is, *Show me Your glory* (Exodus 33:18). Yes, and the glad confidence in which we rest is this: *As for me, I shall behold Your face in righteousness; I will be satisfied with Your likeness when I awake* (Psalm 17:15). This is our desire – a divine and blessed ambition in which there is no pride, no presumption, and no excess! Nothing less can satisfy than the most direct, fullest vision of incarnate glory. Self-emptied before the infinite Majesty, and aware of being completely unworthy even of a servant's place, we still feel as if drawn irresistibly into the innermost circle and center, satisfied with nothing less than *the fullness of Him who fills all in all* (Ephesians 1:23).

The glory which You have given Me I have given to them (John 17:22). According to the promise of the Lord, the glory in reserve is no less than this, both in kind and amount. He delivers over to them the glory given to Him! They become *partakers of Christ* (Hebrews 3:14), and all that He has is theirs. He says, *I have given*, as if it were already theirs by His gift, just as truly as it was His by the Father's gift. He receives it from the Father only for the purpose of immediately handing it over to them! So even here they can say, "This glory is already mine, and I must live as one to whom such infinite glory belongs." *Beholding as in a mirror the glory of the Lord, [they] are being transformed into the same image from glory to glory* (2 Corinthians 3:18). To agonize or despond is sad inconsistency in one who can say, even under severest pressures, *I consider that the sufferings of this present time are not worthy to be compared with the glory that is to be revealed to us* (Romans 8:18). Look at them by themselves, and they do seem at times most overwhelming, but if you place them side by side with the eternal glory, they disappear.

The riches of His glory, says the apostle in one place (Romans 9:23). In another place he says, *The riches of the glory of His inheritance in the saints* (Ephesians 1:18). These are strange expressions! They carry us up to a height of such infinite glory and joy that we feel mystified and overwhelmed. Just as there are riches of grace, riches of mercy, riches of love, and riches of wisdom, so there are riches of glory. It is glory in abundance that will make us rich indeed. The glory spreads over our whole inheritance so that we will have everything and an abundance (Philippians 4:18). This glory is that which God considers His riches and the perfection of His inheritance – the very essence of its beauty and its blessedness.

The freedom of the glory of the children of God, the apostle writes (Romans 8:21), thereby telling us that there is a glory that is the distinct property of the saints – a glory that we can say is our own, thereby distinguishing it from the glory of all other creatures. This glory contains freedom. It sets free those who possess it. Corruption had brought with it chains and bondage, but glory brings with it divine liberty! It is not the liberty that brings the glory, but it is the glory that brings the liberty. Blessed liberty! Freedom from every bondage – not only the bondage of corruption and sin

Blessed liberty!

and death, but the bondage of sorrow, for is not sorrow a bondage? Are not its chains sharp and heavy? The glory sets us eternally free from this bondage of tribulation. It is the last chain, except that of the grave, that is struck from our bruised limbs – but when it is broken, it is broken forever!

This liberty that the glory brings to us is one that will extend to the unconscious creation around us. We brought that creation into bondage, covering it with dishonor and making it the prey of corruption. It now groans and travails under this bitter bondage (Romans 8:22), but just as it has shared our bondage, so it is also to share our liberty; and that same glory that brings liberty to us will introduce the oppressed and dishonored creation into the same blessed freedom! O longed-for fulfillment! O joyful hope! O welcome day, when the Bringer of this glory will arrive, and the voice will be heard from heaven saying, *Behold, I am making all things new* (Revelation 21:5).

It is not only liberty that this glory contains in it, but power also, as it is written, *Strengthened with all power* according to the power of His glory (Colossians 1:11). Even now, this glory has a power-giving energy whereby we are strengthened *for the attaining of all steadfastness and patience* (Colossians 1:11). Thus exulting *in hope of the glory of God* (Romans 5:2), we are prepared for all manner of tribulation and endurance. Though still among the things *not seen* (2 Corinthians 4:18), it not only sends forward a radiance that brightens our path, but it also rains down a strength that enables us to *run with endurance the race that is set before us* (Hebrews 12:1). And so, in an unholy world, we *walk in a manner worthy of the God who calls [us] into His own kingdom and glory* (1 Thessalonians 2:12), having that prayer fulfilled in us: *The God of all grace, who called you to His eternal glory in Christ, will Himself perfect, confirm, strengthen and establish you* (1 Peter 5:10).

Christ in you, the hope of glory (Colossians 1:27). An indwelling Christ is our assurance, our pledge, our hope of glory. Having Him, we have all that is His, whether present or to come. He is the link that binds together the here and the hereafter. We died with Him, we went down into the tomb with Him, we rose with Him, and our life is now *hidden with Christ in God* (Colossians 3:3); but *when Christ, who is our life, is revealed, then [we] also will be revealed with Him in glory* (Colossians 3:4).

The joy with which we rejoice is a *joy inexpressible and full of glory* (1 Peter 1:8), or more literally, it is a "glorified joy." It is a joy such as Paul had when he was caught up into paradise (2 Corinthians 12:2-4). It is a joy such as John had when placed in a vision within sight of the celestial city (Revelation 21-22). It is a joy into whose very essence the thoughts of glory enter. It is a joy that makes the soul that possesses it feel as if it were already surrounded with glory, as if it had *come to Mount Zion and to the city of the living God, the heavenly Jerusalem, and to myriads of angels, to the general assembly and church of the firstborn who are enrolled in heaven* (Hebrews 12:22-23).

The apostle Paul refers to the glorious gospel of Christ (2 Corinthians 4:4) and to *the glorious gospel of the blessed God* (1 Timothy 1:11); or more literally, "the gospel of the glory of Christ" – that is, "the good news about the glory of Christ" and "the good news about the glory of the blessed God." As it is *the gospel of the kingdom* (Matthew 4:23), or good news about the kingdom, that is preached, so it is good news about the glory. God has sent this good news, and is still sending it, to this world. In believing it and receiving God's record concerning the glory, we become partakers of it, and continue to be so – *if we hold fast the beginning of our assurance firm until the end* (Hebrews 3:14). This good news most fully meets our case, no matter how sad or sinful, and shines light into our souls – even in their darkest and most disheartening hours.

Our present light affliction, which is but for a moment, *is producing for us an eternal weight of glory far beyond all comparison* (2 Corinthians 4:17). Therefore, that glory is not merely the issue of tribulation, but is in some sense its product. Tribulation is the soil, and glory is the blossom and the fruit. The soil is rough and unattractive, but the produce is completely perfect. It may seem strange that out of such a field there would grow vegetation so fresh and fruit so divine, yet we know that such is the case. How much we owe to that unlikely soil! Not only do all things work together for good to us, but they as truly work together for glory.

Faith lays hold of this and prizes tribulation, and even glories in it, so realizing the joy as to lose sight of the sorrow, except as contributing to the joy. It is so absorbed in the glory as to forget the shame, except in so far as it is the parent and precursor of the glory.

It is most necessary for us to realize these prospects, these glimpses that God has given us of what we are yet to be. It is not merely lawful to do so for the relief of the heavy-laden spirit, but it is most vitally important to do so for the health of our soul, for our growth in grace, and for enabling us to press on with cheerful energy in the path of service toward God and in usefulness to our brother saints or fellowmen.

The Man of Sorrows had joy set before Him, and it was for this that He *endured the cross, despising the shame* (Hebrews 12:2). He needed it, and so do we, for both He who sanctifies and those who are sanctified are all from one Father (Hebrews 2:11). He found in it strength to bear the cross and endure the shame. So may we, for just as the path He walked is the same that is given us to walk on, so the strength is to be found where our Forerunner found it. There is joy in store for us, even as for Him – joy that is not only like His own, but it is His own very joy (John 15:11). This makes us

willing to bear the cross in all its weight and rough-
ness, and it even lightens it so that often we do not feel
its pressure. We can glory both in the cross and in the
shame. We have less of these than He had, and we have
all His consolation and all His joy to the full.

When this is lost sight of, selfish despondency often
fastens on us. We fret over our griefs until they engross
us entirely, shutting out all else. We magnify them. We
spread them out and turn them over on every side in
order to find out the gloomiest. We take credit to ourselves
for endurance, and thus feed our
pride and self-importance. We
agonize under them, and at the
same time grow vain at being the

*We can glory both in the
cross and in the shame.*

objects of so much sympathy – at having so many eyes
upon us and so many words of comfort addressed to us.

Nothing can be unhealthier than this state of soul.
Nothing is more unlike that in which God expects a
saint to be. It shuts us into the narrow circle of self.
It contracts as well as distorts our vision. It distorts
our spiritual tastes, it lowers our spiritual tone, and it
withers and shrivels up our spiritual being – making
us unfit for all duties of calm and gentle love, and even
hindering the proper discharge of plain and common
duty. It is in itself a serious disease, and it is the source
of other diseases without number.

To respond to this unhealthy tendency, God seeks
to draw us out of ourselves. He does so by holding up
the cross for us to look upon and be healed, but He also
does this by exhibiting the crown and throne. The cross
does not annihilate man's natural concern for self, but

it loosens our thoughts from this by showing us, upon the cross, the One to whose care we may safely entrust self with all its interests, and in whose pierced hands it will be far better provided for than in our own. So the vision of the glory does not make away with self, but it absorbs it and elevates it by revealing the kingdom in which God has made such blessed and enduring provision for us so as to make it appear worse than foolishness in us to fret over our situation and to make self the object of our sad and anxious care. If we are to have glory as surely and as easily as the lilies have their clothing or the ravens have their food, why be so concerned about self? Why think about self at all, except to remember and to rejoice that God has taken all our concerns into His own keeping for eternity?

He takes us by the hand and leads us, as a father does for his child...

Thus God coaxes us away from our griefs by giving us something else to reflect upon – something more worthy of our thoughts. He allures us from the present, where all is dark and unlovely, into the future, where all is bright and beautiful. He takes us by the hand and leads us, as a father does for his child, out from the gloomy ground that we are sadly wandering upon with our eye upon the ground, intent only upon nourishing our sorrows, into fields where all is fresh and Eden-like, so that before we are aware, joy, or at least the soft reflection of it, has crept into our hearts and lifted up our heavy eyes. He does not want us to always abide in the cemetery, or to always sit upon the ground beneath which love is buried, as if the tomb to which we are clinging were our hope, and not the resurrection beyond it. He wants us to come forth – and having led us away from that scene of death, He directs us to look upward, admonishing us for our unbelief and foolishness, and saying to us, "Those whom you love are on the other side. Before long, He who is their life and yours will appear, and you will rejoin each other, each of you embracing, not a weeping, unhealthy fellow mortal, but a glorified saint, set free from pain and sin."

There is nothing healthier and more pleasant for the soul than these anticipations of the morning, and of morning's glory. They are not visionary, except in the sense in which faith is *the assurance of things hoped for, the conviction of things not seen* (Hebrews 11:1). They convey the life of heaven through us, either, on the one hand, making our weak pulse to beat more swiftly, or on the other hand, causing our frenzied pulse to beat more calmly and evenly. They act as regulators of the soul in its wild and unsteady movements, neither allowing us to sink too low nor to soar too high. They tend to steady our extreme impulses by acting as a counterbalance to the weight of grief that so crushes us with its pressure.

These anticipations of the coming morning withdraw us from self and sulking. They widen the circle of our sympathies and throw back into the distance the fence of isolation, which, in times of suffering, we are inclined to put up around ourselves. They suppress mere emotion and forbid us to indulge the flow of grief for its own contentment. They prohibit dismal gloom, which loves to shun out society and chooses loneliness. They fill us with energy for facing the toils, and with ready courage for facing the dangers of the night. They enliven us with the calm but invincible confidence of hope, a hope that expands and brightens as its object approaches.

The morning! That is our watchword. Our evening prayers and songs are filled with it. It gives the hue to life, imparting color to that which is colorless, and freshening that which is faded. It is the essence and term of our hopes. Nothing else will suffice for us or for our world – a world over which the darkness gathers thicker as the years run out. Stars may help to make the sky less gloomy, but they are not the sun – and besides, clouds have now covered them so that they are no longer visible. The firmament is almost without a star. Torches and beacon lights do not help. They make no impression upon the darkness; it is so deep, so real, so unmistakable.

We might give up all for lost if we were not assured that there is a sun and that it is hastening to rise. The church's pilgrimage is nearly done, yet she is not less a pilgrim as its end draws near. No, but she is even more so. The last stage of the journey is the dreariest for her. Her path lies through the thickest darkness that the world has yet felt. It seems as if it were only by the unsteady blaze of strife that we can now shape our way. It is the sound of falling kingdoms that is guiding us onward. It is the fragments of broken thrones lying across our path that assures us that our route is the true one and that its end is near. Then comes the morning with its songs; and in that morning, a kingdom; and in that kingdom, glory; and in that glory, the everlasting rest, the sabbath of eternity.

Horatius Bonar
A Brief Biography

Born on December 19, 1808, Horatius Bonar was one of eleven children of James Bonar and Marjory Pyott Maitland Bonar. For several generations his ancestors had been ministers of the gospel.

Bonar graduated from the University of Edinburgh where Dr. Thomas Chalmers laid the foundation for solid learning, which continued through the years. This gave Bonar direction and strength during his most impressionable years. He was ordained in 1838 and accepted North Parish, Kelso, as his first parish. In addition to Dr. Chalmers, he allied himself with William C. Burns and Robert Murray McCheyne as spiritual mentors and friends.

As a young pastor, Bonar preached in villages and farmhouses throughout his district, for he saw evangelization in a different light from his other contemporaries. To him, Christ had to come first, not numbers of converts. In his house-to-house visitation, he proved himself as a comforter of the sorrowful and a guide for the confused. Colossians 3:23 was the verse he lived by: *Whatsoever ye do, do it heartily, as to the Lord, and not unto men.*

In 1843, he joined the Free Church of Scotland after the "Disruption." The old church with its civil service pastors had failed to arouse the faith of the nation. This disruption was a schism in the Church of Scotland where about 450 evangelical ministers broke away over an issue of the church's relationship with the state. There was disagreement about whether the church was sovereign within its own domain with Christ as Head or if the king was head. In this way, it was similar to the Lutheran Reformation.

Those who left forfeited their livelihood, pulpits, and aid from the established church to found and finance a new national church from scratch. They needed to train clergy and form a new college, which opened in 1843, with Dr. Chalmers as the first principal. Most of the protest principles were conceded by Parliament by 1929, which paved the way for reunification.

In 1843, Horatius Bonar married Jane Catharine Lundie. Together they had nine children, but five of them died before adulthood – three in infancy. One surviving daughter was later widowed with five children, so she moved back with her parents. Horatius said, "God took five children from life some years ago, and He has given me another five to bring up for Him in my old age."

In 1851, he wrote *Man: His Religion and His World* because he was concerned that pastors were diluting the gospel to make it pleasant and easier to accept. He always contended for the truth and never neglected pastoral work and preaching.

Horatius Bonar received an honorary degree of Doctor of Divinity from the University of Aberdeen and then visited Palestine on a mission to the Jews in 1856, which gave him the inspiration for the hymn "The Voice from Galilee," better known as "I Heard the Voice of Jesus Say." Revival had sprung up in Scotland while he was away, and he came back with a renewed interest in prophecy and a firm belief in the personal coming and reign of Jesus Christ. He did not believe that the world was getting better and civilization could save the world. Teachings of the coming of Christ, the tribulation, and the thousand-year reign had been lost, and the nineteenth-century preachers had to bring these doctrines back.

Bonar spoke as a dying man to dying men, resulting in many conversions. He wrote the *Kelso Tracts* to warn the careless, to present salvation simply, and to edify the saints. The tracts had wide circulation in Scotland, England, and America. In 1867, Bonar moved to Edinburgh to take over Chalmers' Memorial Church, and in 1883, he was elected moderator of the General Assembly of the Free Church of Scotland. Bonar continued to express his views in *Prophetical Landmarks* (1847) and served as editor of *The Quarterly Journal of Prophecy* (1848-1873) and the *Christian Treasury* (1859-1879). He even wrote biographies of ministers like *The Life of the Rev. John Milne of Perth* and *The Life and Works of the Rev. G. T. Dodds.*

Other books and tracts that bear his name are *Night of Weeping*, *The Everlasting Righteousness*, and *How Shall I Go to God?* Until his death, he warned about trends he saw creeping in and threatening the Christian church. In one of his last books – *Our Ministry: How It Touches the Questions of the Age* – he observed that "Man is now thinking out a Bible for himself, framing a religion in harmony with the development of liberal thought, constructing a worship on the principles of taste and culture, and shaping a God to suit the expanding aspirations of the age."

Horatius Bonar is best known as the principle hymn writer of Scotland. He was called the "prince of Scottish hymn writers." As he worked with young people, he realized they lacked enthusiasm. Even though he lacked an ear for music, he knew familiar tunes and wrote new words to them for the children. His experiment worked and the children became interested in the verses that were written for them personally. Because they were full of sound teaching, many adults loved to sing them also and requested to use them in other churches. He always granted permission for any church to use his hymns as long as they did not change his words.

He wrote more than six hundred hymns, and many hymnbooks carry these songs. Several are completely compiled from his hymns. The three volumes of *Hymns of Faith and Hope* contain a multitude of his hymns. While "I Heard the Voice of Jesus Say" and "My Redeemer Liveth" were two of the best known, he is largely remembered for his hymns that were based strongly on theology and doctrine, such as "Done is the Work That Saves" and "No Blood, No Altar Now." He wrote of justification, sanctification, the second coming, and the exaltation of Christ.

His hymns are childlike yet manly, hopeful but sympathetic. For many years they were mostly used by churches of other denominations but not his own. The Free Church of Scotland was opposed to singing at worship anything but metrical psalms and paraphrases.

Bonar believed "life is a journey, not a home; a road, not a city of habitation." He stated that "It is not the opinions that man needs; it is truth. It is not theology; it is God. It is not religion; it is Christ. It is not literature and science; but the knowledge of the free love of God in the gift of His only begotten Son." From the first day of his ministry until his last sermon, he closed with these words: "In such an hour as ye think not, the Son of Man cometh."

Other Similar Titles

The Night of Weeping,
by Horatius Bonar

It was God's purpose from the beginning not merely to redeem sinners from His condemnation but also to bring those people into a special relationship with Himself. It is His desire to draw mankind closer to Himself than any other of His creatures and to establish a most special link between His people and Himself.

Since we know that God has our best intentions in mind, what should move us? What can ruin our joy? Our rejoicing is in the Lord, and He is good and has good plans for us. We know that this current life is not our rest, nor do we wish it were, for it is polluted; but our joy is this, that Jehovah is our God, and His promised glory is our inheritance forever. We are being molded and shaped into a vessel fit for His Kingdom!

Available where books are sold.

Follow the Lamb
by Horatius Bonar

Your "turning" or "conversion" is only a beginning, and no more. It is not the whole journey; it is merely the first step. You are a disciple, that is, one who is under teaching; but your teaching, your discipleship, has only *just begun*. Your life is a book; it may be a bigger or smaller volume, but conversion is only the title page or the preface. The book itself remains to be written, and your years, weeks, and days are its chapters, pages, and lines. It is a book written for eternity; make sure that it is written well. It is a book for the inspection of enemies as well as friends; be careful of every word. It is a book written under the eye of God; let it be done reverently, not frivolously, but also without constraint or terror.

Available where books are sold.